MATHEMATiZiNG

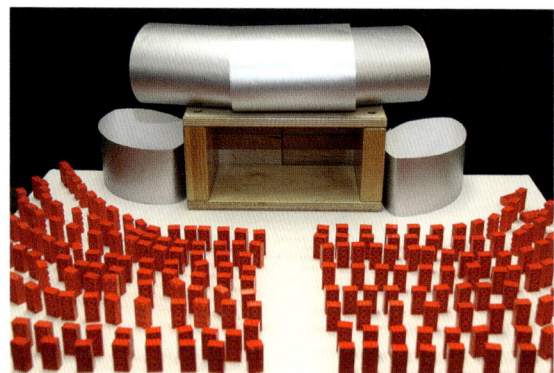

MATHEMATiZiNG

An Emergent Math Curriculum Approach for Young Children

ALLEN C. ROSALES

www.redleafpress.org
800-423-8309

Published by Redleaf Press
10 Yorkton Court
St. Paul, MN 55117
www.redleafpress.org

© 2015 by Allen C. Rosales

All rights reserved. Unless otherwise noted on a specific page, no portion of this publication may be reproduced or transmitted in any form or by any means, electronic or mechanical, including photocopying, recording, or capturing on any information storage and retrieval system, without permission in writing from the publisher, except by a reviewer, who may quote brief passages in a critical article or review to be printed in a magazine or newspaper, or electronically transmitted on radio, television, or the Internet.

First edition 2015
Cover design by Percolator
Cover illustration by Allen David Rosales
Interior design by Percolator
Typeset in ITC Stone Informal
Interior photos by Allen C. Rosales
Printed in the United States of America
22 21 20 19 18 17 16 15   1 2 3 4 5 6 7 8

Library of Congress Cataloging-in-Publication Data

Rosales, Allen C.
  Mathematizing : an emergent math curriculum approach for young children / Allen C. Rosales. — First edition.
     pages cm
  Includes bibliographical references and index.
  ISBN 978-1-60554-395-6 (pbk.)
  ISBN 978-1-60554-396-3 (ebook)
 1. Mathematics—Study and teaching (Elementary) I. Title.
  QA135.6.R65 2015
  372.7'043—dc23
                            2015006439
Printed on acid-free paper

*To my family, for their love and support that has made me
a better educator, husband, and father.*

*To the teachers in our field who are the children's champions.
Your love and perseverance for the work with children
is inspirational.*

*To my Creator, for providing such a masterfully designed
and mathematically patterned creation. Thank you.*

CONTENTS

Acknowledgments

ix

Introduction: What Is Mathematizing?

1

CHAPTER 1: The Mathematizing for Learning Process Approach Theoretical Base

11

CHAPTER 2: Observation Component

17

CHAPTER 3: Exploration with Materials Component

25

CHAPTER 4: Language Modeling Component

43

CHAPTER 5: Inquiry Component

69

CHAPTER 6: Conclusion

115

Glossary

119

Bibliography

123

Index

135

ACKNOWLEDGMENTS

I would like to express my sincere gratitude to the many early childhood schools and educators that have been a part of my personal and professional life and who supported me throughout the writing of this book. The collaboration and friendship that you demonstrated were fundamental to my work, and your dedication to the children and families you serve is inspirational. The following schools opened their hearts and resources to me and played an important part in my ability to apply the Mathematizing for Learning Process approach in their settings. They include: Belmont-Cragin Early Childhood Center, Albany Park Community Center, Chinese American Service League, Erie Neighborhood House, Josiah L. Pickard Elementary School, Carole Robertson Center for Learning, Family Home Daycare, and Laurance Armour Day School.

A special thanks to Reggio Emilia approach practitioners in Italy and the United States for their ability to create spectacular learning environments for children and for sharing their perspectives with the field. I became a Reggio Emilia-inspired practioner in the mid '90s after watching *To Make a Portrait of a Lion* and have followed their work ever since. Thank you for your commitment to the field.

I am also grateful to Erikson Institute's Early Math Collaborative team for their excellent work with early childhood schools in Chicago and for allowing me to participate in the collaborative as a coach and consultant. The math professional development, research, and dissemination practices I experienced in the collaborative strengthened my math practices and inspired me to share those perspectives with the field.

A special thanks to my editors Todd R. Berger, David Heath, Douglas Schmitz, and everyone at Redleaf Press for their patience, collaboration, and professionalism.

Lastly, I give a heartwarming thank-you to all of the teachers, children, and families that allowed me to observe and document their learning practices and processes. I hope my documentation work in this book captured the essence of the mathematizing interactions you experienced at your schools.

INTRODUCTION

WHAT IS MATHEMATIZING?

My earliest recollection of mathematizing—although I didn't realize what was happening at the time—occurred at a grocery store when I was five. My mother engaged me in a fun learning experience while shopping for fruit. "I wonder how many bananas we will need for the week?" she asked me. "Should we buy the big cantaloupe or the small one? Which fruit do you think is heavier, the cantaloupe or the orange? Why do you think the cantaloupe is heavier?" Using words like "how many," "big," "small," and "heavier" as we shopped was my mother's way of introducing mathematizing into my young life. The continual math play we engaged in helped me develop the ability to see and think about math (mathematize) as part of my everyday experiences.

According to *Merriam-Webster's Collegiate Dictionary*, 11th edition, to mathematize is "to reduce to mathematical form." In their *National Council for the Teaching of Mathematics News Bulletin* article, Jacqueline Leonard and Nora Ramirez define mathematizing as "the ability to identify the relationships and quantities that exist in specific contexts" (Leonard and Ramirez 2009, 1). As an early childhood educator, I define mathematizing as "the process of understanding math within the contexts of children's daily lives." The intention with my definition of mathematizing is to direct attention to the words "process," "understanding," and "context," which are key elements of respectful early childhood curriculum practices. This process can be cognitive or linguistic or both.

The grocery store shopping experience I had with my mother is a good example of how a common situation can be reduced to pure mathematical form, in order to teach critical math concepts within a child's context. Teachers can also develop young children's mathematical thinking and provide meaningful math experiences by establishing micro-math cultures in their classrooms. A micro-math culture is a group of classrooms or individuals that share common thoughts, values, and behaviors. Micro-math cultures can be seen as environments, both physical and intellectual, that are created to bring mathematics alive for children. Teachers who establish micro-math cultures in their classrooms mathematize daily routines, activities, play, explorations, and investigations that children encounter through relationships with their friends, families, and environments.

Within any chosen task or activity, mathematizing teachers can help children make sense of the math concepts they are learning. Take for example infant and toddler children who love to fill and dump water into cups, bowls, and other containers at the water table. A teacher with a mathematizing eye observes and identifies the mathematics that the children are investigating, in this instance the concept of conservation and its accompanying variables (volume, capacity, adding, subtracting). Adults can promote critical thinking by having children explore water with cups, sponges, and many other tools and materials. Teachers can also support children's linguistic development by incorporating language-modeling techniques such as labeling, expanding/extending language, and parallel and spiral talking (see chapter 4) to help children develop language and conversation skills. A teacher's math language at the water table could include statements such as these:

- "You are pouring the water into the cup!"
- "You are squeezing the sponge and filling the cup!"
- "The cup is full!"
- "You are dumping the water from your cup!"
- "Your cup is empty now. The water is all gone!"

At the preschool level, the same mathematical conversations could continue, with the opportunity of including more advanced math vocabulary and inquiry to the exchanges. This will help children develop and make meaning of the math concepts they are investigating. Preschool teachers can use language such as the following:

- "Your cup is half full!"
- "The water is reaching the top of your cup!"
- "I wonder how many cups of water it will take to fill the tall container?"
- "Why do you think it took the same number of cups to fill the tall container and the short, wide container?"

The Mathematizing for Learning Process (MLP) approach (see chapter 1) is an effective framework that can support teachers in their interpretation,

Figure i.1 and *Figure i.2*. Teachers Elvira Mata and Andrea Richard mathematizing children's water explorations at the Laurance Armour Day School in Chicago, Illinois

design, and application of rich mathematical experiences in the classroom. It develops students' math understanding in a natural, yet rigorous process.

To get a sense of how teachers can mathematize experiences within a school setting, let's take a look at two examples from the Belmont-Cragin Early Childhood Center, a public school in Chicago. Teachers engaged children and parents in meaningful math learning experiences as a way to encourage mathematizing at school and at home.

In teacher Lourdes Molina's preschool classroom, children became curious about a rainbow that appeared in the sky one rainy day. The class had a long discussion about rainbows, and Mrs. Molina decided to have the children investigate the topic more in-depth through a long-term study. At first, the children observed and focused on the colors and shapes of a rainbow. This interest led to a recycling project where the children were encouraged to collect items at home based on the colors they identified on the rainbow. Once the materials were collected, children grouped the materials based on color, counted the number of items per set, and created a color-pattern rainbow. Sometime later, as children revisited the rainbow project, Mrs. Molina challenged them to think about the length of the rainbow lines. She asked children to estimate the length of each line and to predict which lines would

Figure i.3. Teacher Lourdes Molina and three children counting and measuring the lines of a clay rainbow

be shorter or longer. To prove and verify children's estimations and predictions, the children were provided with clay in order to recreate the rainbow with a new material. Once completed the students used a tape measure to count and find the total length of each rainbow line. The children compared the results to their initial estimations and shared the outcomes.

In a magnificent display of parent engagement, the Belmont-Cragin Early Childhood Center incorporates a fifteen-minute parent/child learning experience every day at the beginning of class. In all seven preschool classrooms, children and parents enter the rooms ready to engage in lesson activities prepared by the classroom teachers. During this time, the parents direct and guide the learning of their children, while the teachers take on facilitator roles. Figures i.4–i.6 show how parents mathematized their children's experiences by helping them identify the properties and attributes of the natural materials, create shapes and letters, group the items, count the quantities of the materials, and finally chart the items on a graph. The classroom teachers end the fifteen-minute session by modeling how to mathematize a read-aloud with books that parents can check out through their classroom lending library.

Figure 1.4, Figure i.5, and *Figure i.6.* Parents engage their children in mathematizing experiences at the Belmont-Cragin Early Childhood Center in Chicago.

MATHEMATIZING OPPORTUNITIES IN OUR ENVIRONMENTS

Before delving into the MLP approach and how this framework can help you, I want to look at some additional mathematizing opportunities within our environment. This first example can take place in any city with tall buildings. A mathematizing teacher can observe a skyscraper (see fig. i.7) and interpret the kinds of math concepts that could be taught or investigated if this building were to be incorporated within a study or unit lesson. In your mind you can create a list (fig. i.8) of math concepts that can be seen in the skyscraper's structure.

Next you find creative and constructive materials to support the learning of the math concepts you have identified and children's meaning-making process. As the students begin to explore the properties of the materials and commence their construction of the structure, you can observe the children's interactions and look for clues about which math concepts they are interested in investigating. Once you identify children's chosen math concepts, you can generate a second list of key math words you can use as the students create with materials and engage with their classmates (fig. i.9).

Your goal is to ensure that the math learning that transpires through your interactions with students is connected to the concepts the children have chosen to investigate. For example, one child's representation of the Willis Tower with Lego blocks (fig. i.10) was a culminating project based on an interest the child followed for a couple months. As he observed the photo of the skyscraper and revisited the Lego structure, he would add structural details and focus on different math concepts throughout the process. This boy's sequential math focus and construction with Lego blocks during the two-month study included these concepts:

Figure i.7. The Willis Tower in Chicago

MATHEMATIZING PROBABILITIES

Height

Width

Length

Perimeter

Surface Area

Patterns

Counting

Addition

Subtraction

Shapes and Form

Figure i.8.

- Height: Child builds a narrow, tall skyscraper.
- Length and width: Next skyscraper construction becomes longer and wider.
- Height and number sense: Structure becomes taller and child counts the levels of the building.
- Patterns: Child begins to create a structure with a focus on vertical and horizontal lines.
- Area: Child notices and creates surface areas on the building.
- Height and number sense: Antennas are added and counted.
- Multiple math concepts: All math concepts investigated are incorporated in the final Willis Tower representation.

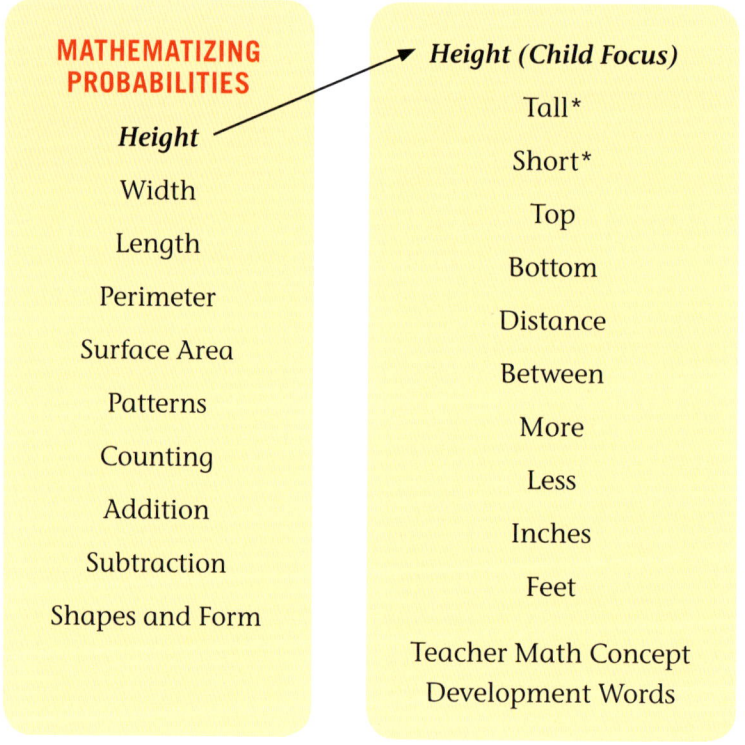

Figure i.9.

Throughout the Willis Tower study, the teacher nurtured mathematical learning by fostering the interests and thinking that emerged from the children's perspectives. This is what differentiates an emergent math curriculum from a traditional skills-based approach to learning mathematics. Emergent mathematics promotes a construction-of-meaning process. Children are provided with real-life contexts and the materials to make sense of the mathematics found within those experiences. The skills-based approach to mathematics, on the other hand, focuses on providing children with an accumulation of factual knowledge with the goal of having them repeat the memorized information. Had the Willis Tower study been incorporated using the skills-based approach, the teacher would have shown the child a photo of the skyscraper and told him everything there was to know about the building. This teacher-directed approach may help in naming parts of the skyscraper, but it does little to develop children's understanding of the mathematics that were incorporated in the construction of the building. In fact, Douglas H. Clements and Julie Sarama, two well-known math-education researchers, state that students may not reach the level of understanding needed for future academic success "if children are not helped to mathematize (reflect on, give language to)" (Clements and Sarama 2014). Mathematizing a tall building and providing the students with many opportunities to create a model of the skyscraper with different materials can help develop a student's understanding of how math is integrated within our environment.

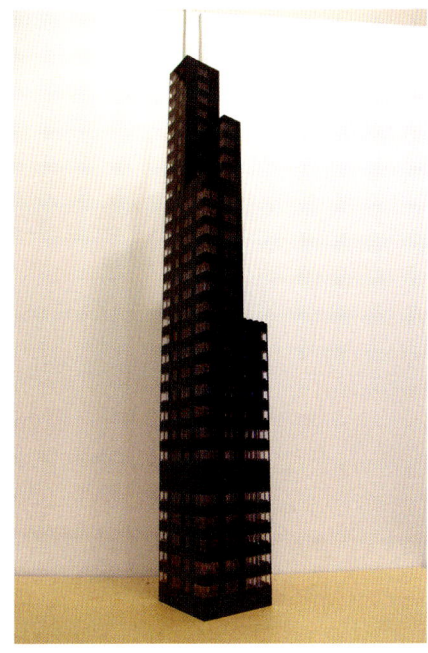

Figure i.10. A five-year-old's representation of the Willis Tower (twenty-eight inches tall) with Legos

Great mathematizing opportunities also occur when teachers use children's environments to promote mathematical learning. Take for example an exuberant tree I photographed in California (fig. i.12). The natural beauty of this tree embodies the essence of rich mathematics existing within living things.

At first glance, some of the mathematical concepts that are visible in the photograph include angles, length, height, and quantity (fig. i.11). A mathematizing teacher interprets the kinds of math concepts that can be investigated with this photograph and plans learning

MATHEMATIZING PROBABILITIES FOR TREE STUDY

Angles

Tall/Short

Wide/Narrow

Far/Near

More/Less

Shapes/Forms

Patterns

Quantities

Proportions

Etc.

Figure i.11.

experiences to help children understand the mathematical relationships between the concepts. After providing meaningful experiences related to the first photograph presented, a teacher can then revisit the tree with photographs taken from different angles. Incorporating this strategy benefits the children in that the new photographs reveal other mathematical concepts that the children can investigate and represent with materials. By supporting children's experiences with this tree study, teachers can ensure the students' work is

- mathematically rich,
- cognitively demanding, and
- promotes worthwhile tasks that "build connections they have not already learned" (Featherstone et. al. 2011, 58).

Figure i.12. First perspective

Figure i.13. Second perspective

Figure i.14. Third perspective

Figure i.15. A five-year-old's drawing of the exuberant tree with pastels

The function, purpose, and goal of mathematizing have evolved over the years. Today it is an in-depth process that integrates the wisdom of parents, teachers, mathematicians, artists, architects, engineers, neuroscientists, and linguists to develop innovative practices. The MLP approach functions as a curriculum and instruction design framework that helps teachers create meaningful learning experiences for children. Its main purpose is to develop students' higher-level thinking and linguistic skills through intentional and purposeful interactions. As teachers mathematize children's daily learning experiences, students learn to see and think about the mathematics that exists within children's contexts. This process helps children understand the role of math in their lives. It begins to instill in them a love of mathematics, thereby reaching the goal of developing mathematically confident and proficient students.

The process of teaching mathematics within real-life contexts has proven to be quite difficult for many teachers who may feel a lack of confidence or a certain type of "math fear." This anxiety towards math can be expected as teachers sometimes relate math knowledge to secondary- or college-level processing, which can be daunting. But, for the early childhood teacher, becoming a proficient mathematizing teacher simply means having the knowledge of the math content and processing that occurs at the age level of the children they are working with and then having the ability to implement quality math experiences within the context of children's lives. The MLP approach frames the kinds of skills, knowledge, and processing a teacher needs to implement successful math experiences. The real-life teaching experiences presented in this book can serve as models for learning. The resources provided can help lower the anxiety some teachers may feel when the topic of math arises. The book can promote the development of positive dispositions toward the teaching of mathematics in preschool settings.

I often hear teachers say "math is everywhere" or "math is in everything," and although these statements are true, to understand the patterns, relationships, and mathematical systems of the concepts inside the "everywhere" or "everything" is the challenge. I wrote this book to provide teachers with a systematic approach to creating and engaging children in rich mathematical experiences. By *rich* I mean experiences that integrate great environmental settings, creative learning materials, and meaningful teacher/child interaction. Rich experiences focus on the mathematics that exists within the topics being explored or investigated by the children. The MLP approach components can help teachers see and interpret the math inside the "everywhere" or "everything," and support teachers as they develop curricula for their students.

This book is intended to

- provide a practical mathematizing approach for teachers working with very young children;
- present vivid examples, processes, and illustrations of great math processing in early childhood settings;
- present creative strategies and techniques for teachers to develop their pedagogical skills; and
- promote and develop teachers' and children's mathematical and multidimensional thinking and processing skills.

This is the kind of mathematical thinking and processing that is in high demand worldwide and "that develops students' abilities to deal with complex systems" (English 2011b, 1).

The methods, strategies, and techniques in this book can be used by teachers to develop their teaching skills. The four components in the MLP approach framework (observation, exploration, language modeling, and inquiry) constitute fundamental skills teachers need in order to implement high-level interactions with children. In my work with early childhood programs, I've found that centers that incorporated this framework within long-term professional learning communities saw the greatest increases in the quality of their curriculum and instructional practices. The teachers were able to change their "math fear" into "math confidence" and learned to provide intentional and purposeful math experiences to the children in their care.

Now that we have seen some mathematizing possibilities in our environments and settings, let's take a look at the MLP approach.

1
The Mathematizing for Learning Process Approach Theoretical Base

The Mathematizing for Learning Process (MLP) approach is an emergent math curriculum and instructional framework that focuses on four fundamental teaching and learning components. Together, these four components create dynamic learning experiences for children:

- **Observation** is when the teacher observes and interprets the children's interests in order to create and incorporate engaging mathematical learning experiences for them.

- **Exploration** promotes the learning that emerges from the creative process.

- **Language modeling** provides teachers with math, grammar, and language techniques to help them engage children in meaningful conversations.

- **Inquiry** provides teachers with systematic procedures and strategies for developing children's higher-level thinking.

Chapters 2 through 5 will explore each of these four components in depth.

Influenced by the work of Jean Piaget, Lev Vygotsky, John Dewey, Howard Gardner, Loris Malaguzzi, and Jim Cummins, the MLP approach framework aligns with many of the key principles shared by progressive educators. These teachers believe that children learn best when the learning is individualized, social, and within a real-world context. The design of the MLP approach is guided by the following principles and values:

- children choosing their own learning contexts
- the importance of play
- language acquisition and development
- critical thinking
- collaboration

Mathematizing for Learning Process Approach Framework

1 **Observe**	2 **Explore Materials**	3 **Language Model**	4 **Provide Inquiry**
• Find Rich Context and the Optimum Learning Opportunity • Identify the Environmental, Role-playing, and Representational Contexts/Interests • Recognize Physical Movements/Actions • Describe Indirect/Direct Math Processing Occurring in the Moment	• Instill Curiosity with Creative and Constructive Materials • Discover the Physical Properties and Attributes of Materials • Create, Represent, and Play to Develop Multi-Dimensional Thinking Skills	• Develop Math Grammar • Label, Expand, and Extend Language • Parallel and Spiral Talk • Engage in Ongoing, Sustained, and In-Depth Conversations	• Promote Creative and Critical Thinking through Holistic, Integrated Projects • Implement High-Level Questioning Patterns to Develop Problem Solving, Reasoning, and Proof Skills • Create Protocols to Establish a Group Metacognition and Reflective Practice Culture

Figure 1.1.

CHILDREN CHOOSING THEIR OWN LEARNING CONTEXTS

The first principle is the belief that children have the right to choose their own learning contexts. These include classroom areas, materials, topics, focuses, and learning styles. Take for example a child who enjoys drawing pictures of his family in the art area. A respectful teacher acknowledges this student's topic of interest and materials of choice, and nurtures the learning by developing the classroom area with different materials and providing many opportunities for him to make sense of the concept of family.

Many emergent curriculum models across the early childhood field value this right. These models include the Reggio Emilia approach (Edwards et al.

2011; Vecchi 2010), the project approach (Helm and Katz 2010), the developmental approach to education (Shapiro and Nager 2000), Bilingual Education Models (Baker 2011; Echevarria et al. 2012), and other constructivist education models. Constructivist theorists assert that children construct meaning of information when the new content is connected to prior experience or knowledge. The teacher needs to understand children's cultural background, knowledge, interests, and ideas, and then use that information to plan learning experiences that will support students' intellectual development. Allowing children to choose their learning contexts empowers them to engage meaningfully with the environment the teachers have created for them to enjoy.

Figure 1.2. Five-year-old's representation of family inside his home

THE IMPORTANCE OF PLAY

A second key principle that the MLP approach framework embraces is the important role of play in children's lives. Play in this context includes exploration, investigation, and role playing, where the children use these processes to construct meaning of the world around them. This follows the work of social constructivist theorists (Vygotsky 1978; Dewey 1933; Piaget 1962). Social constructivism asserts that children learn by engaging in collaborative processes with other individuals and their environment. As children explore, create, and express themselves, they begin to develop their logical-mathematical skills—the ability to understand objects' relations concretely and abstractly. For example, when children are provided with many opportunities to play with blocks, they begin to reason and understand (logic) how those objects are constructed and how the parts can be connected (math) to create representations. Play experiences are significant in that children build background knowledge that they can use later in life. When the children encounter abstract mathematical concepts in the elementary grades, they will be able to link those new math concepts to the structures they have created and the thinking they have processed during playtime. The play experiences of today support the cognitive and academic learning of tomorrow.

LANGUAGE ACQUISITION AND DEVELOPMENT

Children's right of language acquisition and development is the third principle that this mathematizing framework supports. Theorists have written extensively on how children develop language skills through innate abilities (Chomsky 1965); social contexts and environments (Piaget 1962, 2001; Bates 1976; Vygotsky 1962); and culturally relevant experiences (Cummins 1981). As these language theories and research suggest, children acquire language through their relationships with individuals and interactions with their environment.

When you listen to children's conversations during playtime, you can identify cultural and linguistic learning processing. As they engage in pretend play, children represent the experiences that they encounter in their lives. Teachers that plan intentional activities make a point to interact with children by modeling both social and academic language. The language modeling process helps students make sense of the concepts they are investigating. In particular, academic success has been linked to children's ability to understand and use academic language (Scarcella 2008; Opitz and Guccione 2009; Hakuta et al. 2000). Therefore, it is vital for teachers to increase their own math grammar. They need to be well equipped with language-modeling strategies and techniques to help support children's math language development in a natural and purposeful manner.

CRITICAL THINKING AND COLLABORATION

The principles of critical thinking and collaboration are the final two theoretical elements that influenced the development of the inquiry component of the MLP approach. Assisting children in the process of developing mathematical thinking skills can be a challenge. Teachers need to acquire the knowledge and the tools to support students in constructing meaning. One of the best thinking reference tools in education is Benjamin Bloom's *Taxonomy of Educational Objectives* (1956, 2000). The classification of thinking moves found in Bloom's matrix (pp. 15, 98), which is composed of hierarchical levels (lower- to higher-level thinking), can help teachers engage children in critical thinking experiences based on each student's proficiency level.

The benefits of using Bloom's taxonomy during an inquiry experience can occur, for example, as a teacher is having children compare the lines and shapes of different buildings. This comparative-thinking activity is considered a higher-level process, as it requires students to remember, highlight, and differentiate between key mathematical concepts. If the children are not able to respond during the comparative analysis, the teacher can use Bloom's taxonomy to modify the activity by asking students simpler questions. The difficulty of the inquiry can also move upward if the questions being asked by the teacher are too simple. Knowing and applying Bloom's taxonomy during inquiry experiences can increase students' abilities to think critically about the topics they are investigating. This, in turn, can support the development of independent, competent, thinking individuals.

The principle of collaboration stems from constructivist theory. It proposes that each individual's experience and background knowledge can positively impact the learning outcomes of a group of students working together (Vygotsky 1987). Collaborative elements can encourage teachers to establish environments and atmospheres where children learn to

Bloom's Taxonomy of Educational Objectives

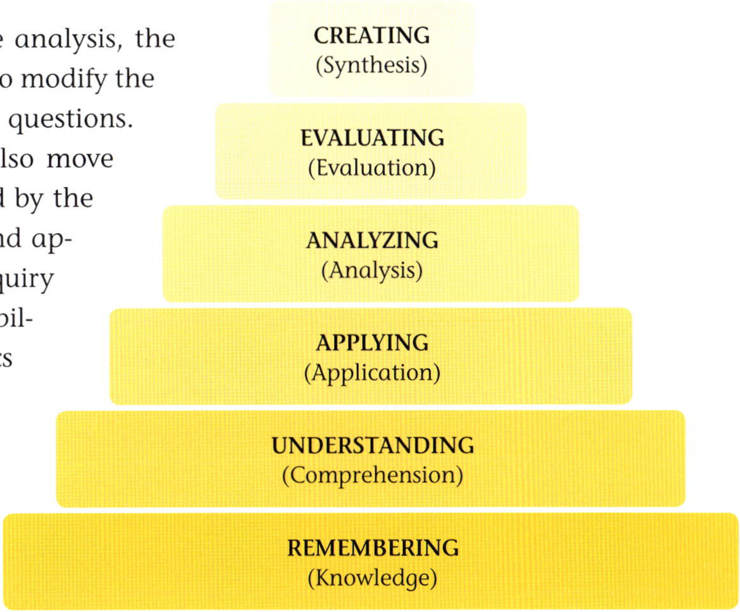

- CREATING (Synthesis)
- EVALUATING (Evaluation)
- ANALYZING (Analysis)
- APPLYING (Application)
- UNDERSTANDING (Comprehension)
- REMEMBERING (Knowledge)

Figure 1.3.

- engage in equitable participation;
- cooperate in perspective sharing;
- share in harmonious dialogue;
- problem solve through a collective experience; and
- produce representations and outcomes that provide "satisfaction" to the group's effort (Vecchi 2010).

Student collaboration can promote democratic classroom cultures that support social justice through shared engagement and group learning. This process can ensure all children are provided with the resources and experiences they need to feel they are an integral part of a community of learners.

Teachers can increase the quality of the collaborative process by implementing *metacognitive processing* (planning how to think about something) and *reflective-practice processing* (thinking and learning from our actions). For instance, as children engage in a project using recycled materials, the group can think about the creative process before, during, and after the experience.

This intentional approach to thinking promotes children's abilities to solve problems, refine processes and products, and instill lifelong thinking skills they can use in other contexts within their lives. Incorporating metacognitive and reflective practice processes can support students' higher-level thinking.

The following chapters of the book present and describe each component of the MLP approach and its accompanying elements. As you read the descriptions of the various elements, it is important to keep in mind that the process can be both static and dynamic. This means that teachers can choose to implement the approach in part or as a whole, based on the specific context. Observation is the only component that must be incorporated in any mathematizing situation, as it sets the teaching stage.

Teachers may decide to *only* observe and have students explore with materials so that the focus is on how children perceive, reason, and create on their own. A teacher may choose to *only* observe and model language based on children's actions so that the focal point is on the development and acquisition of language. A teacher can choose to *only* observe and provide in-depth inquiry with the students during work and play times so that the emphasis is on developing children's higher-level thinking skills. Then again, teachers may decide to use all the mathematizing components simultaneously if they feel the students have the ability to understand and the learning context is appropriate.

Mathematizing for Learning Process Approach Static or Dynamic Options

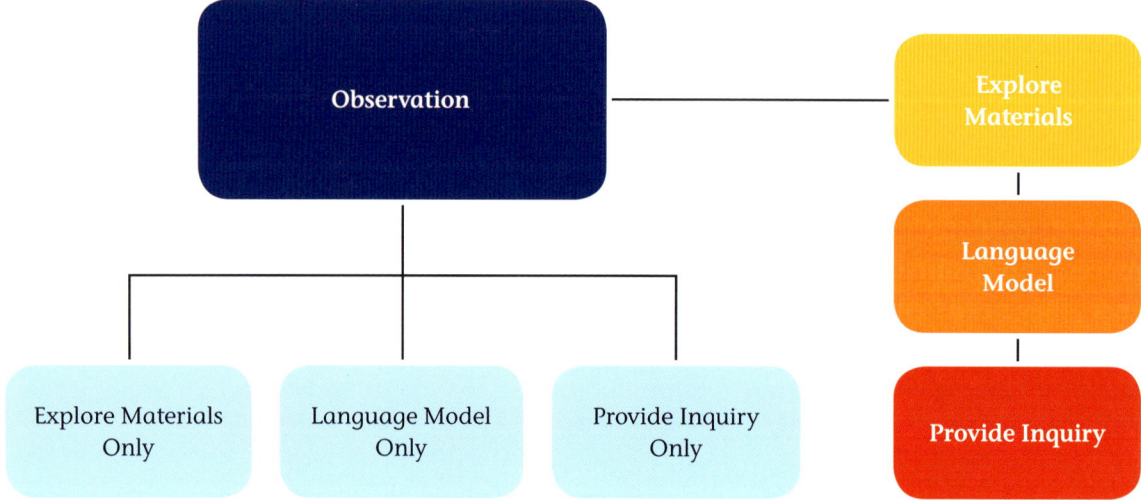

Figure 1.4.

2

Observation Component

Emergent curriculum models of instruction, such as the MLP approach, emphasize learning experiences that "emerge" from the children's interests and perspectives. Teachers who implement emergent curriculum practices begin their educational planning by gathering relevant facts (context) about the children. This includes information such as cultural backgrounds, topics or concepts of interests, favorite learning areas and styles, and other pertinent information that the teacher can use to create the optimal learning opportunity. Students' optimal learning opportunities occur when their hearts and minds are focused on the topics or ideas they have decided to investigate at the moment. Finding rich context as a means for curriculum planning is very important as educational theory tells us that children come to understand new ideas through their personal knowledge and experiences. Using students' contexts and interests to bridge new learning supports them in the process of constructing understanding of the world, which can lead to learning, knowledge, and skills over time. Three elements of the observation component of the MLP approach are meant to help teachers collect meaningful information to plan rich mathematical experiences based on children's interests.

IDENTIFYING ENVIRONMENTAL, ROLE-PLAYING, AND REPRESENTATIONAL CONTEXTS AND INTERESTS

The process of identifying children's environmental, role-playing, and representational contexts and interests is the first mathematizing procedure that a teacher can use. This entails a teacher observing classroom learning experiences to understand the areas and materials children like to play in (environmental), the kinds of character roles the students assume (role-playing), and the creations children make with materials (representational). The information collected through this process helps us understand the optimal learning environments for children so we can design respectful and meaningful curriculum. Let's look at the three identification elements a bit closer.

The environmental settings consist of the various classroom areas and the materials available for students in those spaces. For example, think about observing the environmental setting of a block play area. You can think about the size and dimensions of that area in order to understand potential spatial limitations and then estimate how much the children's block constructions might grow and develop. If a block area is too small, it limits the amount of detail that can be added to the structures being built. You can also assess the quality of the block area's *visual integrity*. This refers to the setup and presentation of the area. Ask yourself questions, such as

- Are there enough materials to support extended play opportunities?
- Does the area have quality photos that depict authentic buildings and structures and that can inspire children's creativity?
- Is the block area welcoming and aesthetically pleasing?

Figure 2.1. A girl creating three-dimensional forms with clay

Additionally, having a deep understanding of the materials available in the classroom areas and how they can be used to create children's structures or works of art can help you plan and incorporate interactions that develop students' math knowledge. For instance, you might observe children engaging with clay. You know that clay can be changed from two-dimensional shapes into three-dimensional forms, so you can guide the children in the creative process. Knowledge of how clay can be manipulated can help you plan for further clay exploration experiences by bringing in more tools and materials to support and extend the children's learning.

Gathering information regarding children's role-play interests is also very important. As you observe children's play scenarios and the characters they pretend to be, you begin to interpret the kinds of mathematical concepts that can be incorporated during the play experience. Teacher Fran Landt's mathematical physics in urban engineering study occurred over a period of five months. During the study, children created a model of their neighborhood school's environment (setting) and took on the roles of surveyors, architects, and engineers. In this learning situation, Landt could add "neighborhood" and "community helpers" to the contextual information list collected during the observation stage of the mathematizing process. The next move would be to find the interests that the children have focused on during their construction and role-play phases.

The third observational procedure a mathematizing teacher processes is identifying the representational interests the children have created. In Landt's classroom, the children chose the neighborhood as the setting and assumed the roles of specific community helpers during their play experiences. However, the *representational interests*, or the objects they decided to create with materials over time, included a bridge, a building, an elevator pulley system, a sidewalk, a road, a school, and a garage. These structures represented the interests that the children had throughout the study, making it clear that the mathematical learning opportunities in this situation could come from the study of buildings and how things functioned in the neighborhood.

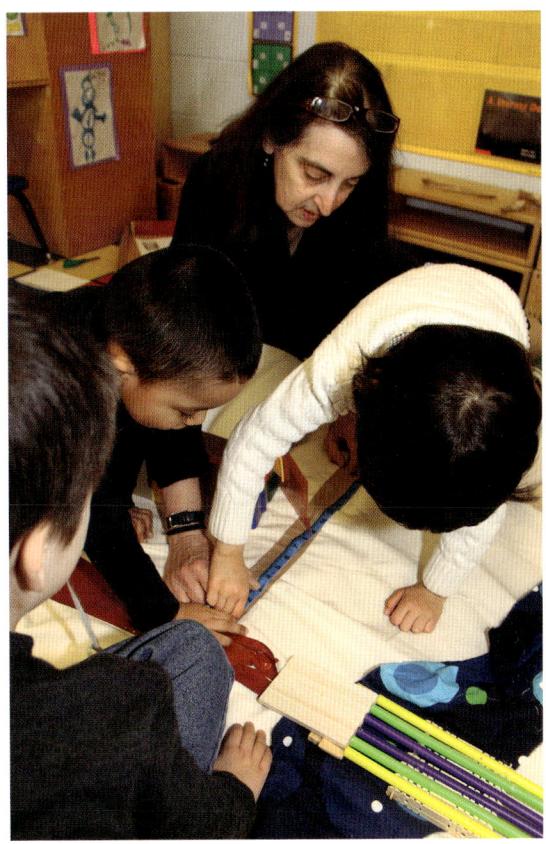

Figure 2.2. Teacher Fran Landt observing and mathematizing children's neighborhood study process

Pinpointing students' contexts and interests through the observation of the environmental, role-playing, and representational aspects in children's play allows you to think about and develop meaningful interactions with students. Understanding these elements provides the rich teaching context through which you can mathematize based on your students' thoughts and interests.

RECOGNIZE PHYSICAL MOVEMENTS AND ACTIONS

The second observational element involves recognizing the physical movements and actions the children are engaged in. Movement of any sort—throwing, measuring, climbing, pouring, drawing—involves math and science processing. Therefore, when teachers observe children's physical movements and actions, they can interpret children's mathematical thinking and nurture those movements with materials, language, and inquiry. This observational process is especially important for interacting with young children birth through age three and with dual-language learners, as their movements provide cues needed to interpret children's mathematical processing and communication.

Two toddler boys at the block area built a structure with foam blocks. They used their arms to construct and their whole bodies to explore the surface areas. However, each child investigated the spaces with different actions. One child was interested in crawling under the structure, while the second was interested in climbing over it. This meant the mathematical concept that each child decided to investigate was different. A mathematizing teacher gathers this information and uses it to interact with the children on the spot with materials and language modeling, or the teacher uses it to shape future learning experiences.

Interpreting the mathematical movements and actions of the children allows you to incorporate cognitive scaffolding and cognitive conflict with the materials available in the interest areas.

Figure 2.3. Toddlers using their bodies to explore spatial relations concepts

- *Cognitive scaffolding* means that the teacher supports children's learning by providing them with materials they can use to solve problems on their own. For instance, when a child is unable to count up to twenty with loose materials, the teacher may provide an abacus to help the child count precisely. In this scenario, the teacher recognized that the student enjoyed using small manipulatives to count; therefore providing an abacus links the fine-motor experience with a more effective tool for counting.

- *Cognitive conflict* is the process of encountering new situations or facts that "conflict" with what we already deem to be true. For example, when a teacher challenges children to predict which eight-ounce cup holds more, the tall, narrow cup or the short, wide cup, they enter into cognitive conflict when they find out that both cups hold the same amount of liquid. As the children investigate the information, critical thinking is used to make sense of the new facts, which in turn promotes cognitive development.

During toddler block play, you can ask yourself questions such as: "What other materials can I provide the children to experience the same movements and actions? How can I set up the environment to promote the mathematical concepts the children decided to investigate? How can I support the kind of play that allows children to connect and understand the mathematical relationships found in structure?" Such guiding questions can help you create and incorporate learning experiences for children that are meaningful and purposeful, cognitively demanding, and mathematically rich. These and many other opportunities arise when you recognize the children's physical movements while playing.

> The Observation Component of the MLP approach helped me interpret and understand the math that the children were processing. When I observed children's investigations with materials, I was able to stay focused on what they were doing with materials, what math concepts were being expressed, and what math vocabulary I could use with them to further their math understanding. —**Master Teacher Meredith Chambers**

DESCRIBE INDIRECT/DIRECT MATH PROCESSING OCCURRING IN THE MOMENT

In a previous observation in a preschool classroom, a child was in the dramatic play area and assumed the role of Goldilocks. She was pretending to cook dinner for the family of bears, so she added food toys into a pot, tasted the food, and stated that it was too hot. The girl began to blow air on the food and continued a conversation focused on the temperature of the food. Finally she tasted the food and stated that it was just right. During this play experience, the girl processed both indirect and direct mathematics. *Indirect processing* occurs when a child uses math processing without focusing on the math concept. In the example, the girl processed math indirectly when she processed the math concepts of volume and quantity as she filled the pot with food toys. *Direct processing* occurs when a child focuses on specific math concepts during an interaction. In the example, the girl talked about and reflected upon the concept of temperature. A mathematizing teacher, therefore, finds the direct math processing that occurs within children's experiences and uses the information to develop meaningful learning opportunities based on the math concepts the children have decided to investigate.

Describing the indirect and direct math processing that the children are experiencing is the third observational element. It is also the most challenging mathematizing observation procedure for teachers. It entails an adult reducing children's contexts to pure mathematical terms. The teacher observes the math processing the children are experiencing with materials and listens to the conversations they are having during the activity. This helps teachers to identify and understand the concepts the children have focused on. Once teachers interpret the math concepts the children are investigating, they can incorporate math language and inquiry, based on the direct math observed, to develop students' knowledge.

A teacher needs a solid understanding of math in order to gather math processing information. A sufficient amount of this information is needed to differentiate between the children's indirect and direct math activity. This is where a teacher's understanding of physical properties (p. 35) and math grammar (pp. 44–51) play a huge role. For example, a mathematizing teacher understands objects have various physical properties (length, height, weight) and that each object can be defined by attributes (sides, angles, tall, short). Once the teacher identifies all the attributes the students are processing, she can interpret which math concepts the children are exploring indirectly and which ones they are investigating directly. When teachers scaffold the learning based on the direct math concepts, they ensure that children stay focused. This respectful practice is a key element and goal for mathematizing teachers, as it sustains children's interests in the learning process.

Look at the photograph of teacher Snejana Tzontcheva as she incorporated a mathematical physics in urban engineering project during her five-month study. Think about the possible math processing that occurred as the children recreated a school building with Lego blocks, Zoobs, a pulley, and rope. Indirectly and directly, the children added, subtracted, measured (height, length, depth, weight), created patterns and forms, and problem-solved the mechanical functions of an elevator. Your role as the mathematizing teacher at this point is to consider all the possible math learning that the children processed. Then based on the evidence, you decide which of the math concepts the students decided to investigate. If you are able to interpret and pinpoint the children's math learning patterns of interest, then you can begin the next mathematizing elements—exploration with materials, language modeling, and inquiry—to support students' intellectual development of those concepts.

Figure 2.4. Teacher Snejana Tzontcheva mathematizing children's building and elevator construction during a math-physics study

In the following mathematical physics in urban engineering study, observe how teacher Rosalinda Carrasquillo from the Albany Park Community Center in Chicago mathematizes children's learning experiences by finding rich context and then developing the mathematical concepts the students decided to investigate.

MATHEMATICAL PHYSICS IN AN URBAN ENGINEERING STUDY

The children had been studying the structures and functions of their neighborhood environment. Teacher Rosalinda Carrasquillo read a book on bridges based on children's interests and opened the project to everyone. Children quickly moved towards a machine they had constructed and wanted to know how objects could be transported to a far location. The group discussed the properties of the materials that Carrasquillo provided and chose some to incorporate in their investigation. The children constructed a ramp and placed it at the tip of the machine. They tested the movement of different objects by rolling them down the ramp and measuring the distance they traveled.

Figure 2.5a. Teacher Rosalinda Carrasquillo reading a book about bridges

Figure 2.5b. Exploring the function of a machine built with recycled materials

Figure 2.5c. Discussing the properties of building materials

Figure 2.5d. Investigating and testing their hypotheses

Figure 2.5e. Presenting the mathematical results

3

Exploration with Materials Component

Exploring, creating, and playing with various types of materials is a fundamental component of the MLP approach. You can support students' mathematical thinking when you use materials designed to promote math thought and create environments that promote creativity and collaboration. Through interactions with creative and constructive materials, children can develop and build math foundations that will help them in future academic settings.

Creative materials can include clay, paint, wire, paper, and elements found in nature, such as sticks, rocks, pinecones, and leaves. They could possess physical properties—plasticity, permeability, adhesion, mass, volume, quantity, and other math and science properties that promote imaginative thinking. Creative materials support the development of *topological thinking*, which is the mathematical ability to think and work with shapes, forms, and space.

Constructive materials can include lumber, blocks, Legos, magna-tiles, PVC pipe, electrical conduit fittings, and boxes. These materials possess physical properties such as strength, elasticity, stiffness, stress, magnitude, and multitude. Constructive materials promote logical thinking and integrate the powerful concept of units in measurement. Constructive materials also develop *modularity*, which is the ability to think and process in standard units and dimensions.

One grand opportunity to provide children with rich math experiences and language can occur as children interact with a creative material such as clay. Clay directly and indirectly allows children to engage in many mathematical processes at the same time. As a child takes hold of a chunk of clay, he will have to separate (divide) the larger chunk into two pieces many times. Then he will take away (subtract) smaller pieces from the larger

Figure 3.1. Teacher Flor Villanueva-Winter's preschool students with their dinosaur representation made with recycled materials

Figure 3.2. Exploring the properties of constructive materials

portions and continue on by putting the smaller pieces back together (adding). Finally he can create more of the same (multiply) creations as he constructs many objects.

Notice how the basic action or process words *separate*, *take away*, *together*, and *more* have the equivalent underlying meaning as your typical elementary math words *divide*, *subtract*, *add*, and *multiply*.

It is important that teachers use age-appropriate language for describing math concepts. A mathematical continuum (fig. 3.3) exists throughout the early childhood years. Understanding the importance of incorporating and developing these processes and using language intentionally is critical for teachers. It is through this awareness that teachers can provide developmentally appropriate, yet advanced, math-learning experiences to all children through what they see the students creating.

Intentional design and construction of inspiring learning spaces in the classroom also supports children's exploration of materials. The early childhood classroom, in any educational setting, is a mathematician's paradise, as many of the materials in the children's areas of interest can be explored and manipulated mathematically. However, teachers can increase children's learning opportunities by setting up environments that provoke curiosity, challenge intuition, and develop critical thinking.

Mathematical Concept and Language Continuum in Early Childhood

Math Concept	Infant/Toddler	Preschool	Elementary
Number Sense	More, all gone, counting numbers, all together . . .	Add, take away, separate, increase, counting numerals, total, zero . . .	Adding, subtracting, dividing, multiplying, digits, sum, integers . . .
Measurement	Big, little, full, empty, hot, cold, heavy, light . . .	Long, tall, short, distance, inches, degree, freezing, cup, large, small . . .	Foot, yard, pint, quart, gallon, ounce, pound, conversation . . .
Geometry	Circle, square, in, out, under, around, up, down . . .	Sphere, cube, cone, pyramid, sides, area, below, perimeter, high, low . . .	Points, lines, angles, planes, rays, vertex, congruent, line segment . . .
Algebra	Again, behind, in front, together, another	Repeat, before, after, next to, sort, first, last, same, different	Order, group, set, linear/growing patterns, constant, variable . . .

Figure 3.3.

One intentional approach to creating engaging environments is to look at each interest area in the classroom and consider the three-dimensional space. Deliberately make use of the length, width, and depth of any area the children are interested in. As you plan to incorporate intentional three-dimensional spaces, think of and include furniture, creative and constructive materials, displays of children's learning experiences, and architectural components (floor, wall, windows, ceiling) available to create dynamic learning spaces for children.

Examples of beautifully created interest areas can be found at the Belmont-Cragin Early Childhood Center in Chicago. Teachers and administrators collaborated on creating three-dimensional interest areas that envelop children's senses immediately when they enter the areas and as they interact with the materials in those spaces. Intentionally designed spaces can promote and encourage mathematical concepts, creative thinking, and student collaboration. When these elements are combined, they can lead to dynamic learning experiences for children and adults.

Figure 3.4. The block area of the Belmont-Cragin Early Childhood Center

The mathematical learning possibilities are endless when you create inspiring spaces and provide children with materials that contain different math and science properties and attributes. The quality of the material that you provide to children will directly affect the quality of children's thinking. Because of this, it is beneficial to provide different materials that can promote cognitively demanding learning and thinking. You need to carefully select the kind of materials you provide to the children. Select materials that "develop a greater awareness of the properties and possibilities in the material" (Scheinfeld et al. 2008, 56) and that promote different types of mathematical activity (Ginsburg 2006). This way you can ensure that the learning experiences help to develop mathematical competence in children "who learn that mathematics makes sense and who learn to trust their own abilities to make sense of it" (Richardson 2003, 321).

Figure 3.5. Preschoolers and their families' representations of vehicles with creative materials

INSTILLING CURIOSITY

Children's curiosity about the world is apparent in their interactions with their environments and the materials available within those environments. As discussed previously, teachers who create authentic and aesthetically pleasing classroom environments can motivate and inspire children to explore and discover the essence of their environments.

Curiosity is essential for any learner beginning on a journey of understanding (Ritchhart et al. 2011). Curiosity is important because it

- promotes an active mind,
- helps us recognize new ideas,
- leads us in the discovery of new possibilities, and
- instills excitement into our lives.

When provided with creative and constructive materials, children often become curious and begin to wonder and think about the different ways the materials can be used. Children's interests, concepts, and ideas emerge when their curiosity is triggered, which motivates students to explore and investigate the materials. Motivation is a catalyst for learning as "spontaneous motivation constitutes a first important spark and a good foundation subsequently for learning processes" (Vecchi 2010, 40). The curiosity and critical thinking that take place as children investigate the materials' properties (and possibilities!) can lead to detailed creations. These representations often demonstrate children's thoughts and ideas about the world around them.

The use of creative arts (literature, performing, media, and visual arts), media (clay, wire, leaves, paper, twigs), and different modalities (hearing, seeing, touching, and moving) to instill curiosity can lead to children's multidimensional thinking (imaginative, intuitive, mathematical, logical). This higher-level skill occurs as children become engaged in a topic of interest and are able to make sense of the content through multiple experiences, lenses, and modalities. As teachers provide opportunities for children to engage in still-life drawings, role playing scenes from a book, creating a structure from a photograph, and other artistic processes, they provide the necessary experiences for students to learn how to problem solve creatively.

Representations of the Reggio Emilia San Prospero Lion

The following learning experiences were provided to a kindergartner and a preschooler to demonstrate how photographs can be used to spark children's curiosity and how materials can be used to create representations of the objects they have become interested in investigating. These learning experiences were inspired by the work of Amelia Gambetti, who was an educator in the Reggio Emilia municipal schools in Italy.

Kindergartner Planning for the Drawing

The child said: "The lion is big. He has lots of lines and shapes. Straight lines, curved lines, diagonal lines. Also, oval shapes and circles shapes. There is shade on his neck, mouth, nose, and eyes. There are long and short lines. The curved lines make a pattern. Light-dark-light-dark. His face has circle patterns, too many for me to count."

Figure 3.6. Reggio Emilia lion statue

Figure 3.7. A kindergartner's first lion representation with drawing paper and pencil

Figure 3.8. The kindergartner's second lion representation using tracing paper and a soft lead pencil

After the Drawing
The child said: "That's a statue of a lion and he's roaring and growling at the moon. He's trying to call all the other lions to eat dinner because dinner is ready. The lion went hunting for food and then he started cooking it for his family. The papa lion went outside after dinner and looked at the moon again. He was thinking about his family. He thinks he should protect his family from predators."

Kindergartner's Second Lion Representation
The child said: "This is cool! I can't believe you can see the lion through the paper! This time I can see more patterns. Now I see lots of dots on the lion's mane and on his face. There are also patterns of light and shade. I think I will trace the outer part of the lion's face, and then I can trace the long and short curved lines I see on him. After I finish the lines I will fill in all the shapes where I see shade."

Kindergartner's Third Lion Representation
The child said: "This is the lion's castle. I built tall walls and there are patterns on top of the castle, open-close-open-close, and brick patterns on the side. The castle is for the lion and his family so they can be safe from predators. There is no way the bad guys will get inside the castle because there's an invisible bridge that opens and closes so the predators are going to think there are no doors and they will hit the invisible brick bridge and they are going to be destroyed and the family will be safe."

Figure 3.9. The lion's castle made with clay: eleven inches long by eight inches wide by six inches high

Preschooler Planning for the Drawing

The three-year-old child said: "I see diagonal lines, circles for the eyes and mouth. It's my project and I want to draw up and down and I draw a C because his face is a C shape. And I want to draw lots of Js because it's on the lion's mane."

After the Drawing

The child said: "The lion is hunting for food. He's roaring because he's chasing the hyenas because hyenas are bad. The hyena was chasing the baby lion so the big papa lion chased the hyena away."

Preschooler's Second Lion Representation

While tracing, the preschooler commented: "I can trace the lines through the paper. Look! I can see it. I see lots of lines and shades. This line is a J because it curves. One line, two lines, three, four, five, . . . forty, forty-one, forty-two, . . . seventy, seventy-one, seventy-two. Hey, that's too many lines. Why can't it be one hundred already? I'm not doing more than ninety-nine lines. No, I'm going to shade now; that was too many lines. There, I shade his mouth, neck, nose, and eyes. Wait, I forgot the moon. Okay, I'm done."

Preschooler's Third Lion Representation

The preschooler said: "I made this cave so the lion can keep his family safe. Two baby lions were in the hyena's cave and the papa lion went inside to save them. He hit the hyenas and destroyed them. Then he told the baby lions to go back into the lion cave with their mommy."

Figure 3.10. A preschool child's first lion representation with drawing paper and pencil

Figure 3.11. Preschooler's second lion representation with tracing paper and a soft lead pencil

Figure 3.12. Preschooler's third lion representation using clay

The Reggio Emilia square lion photograph stimulated both children's curiosity about the lion's thinking and actions. They used their imaginations and knowledge to understand the context and the content of the situation. Both children used creative and critical thinking skills as they generated ideas to play with the creative materials; processed and created things that demonstrated their thinking; and spoke with gestures to explain their ideas and reasoning. In this study about a lion, curiosity, along with the teacher's introduction of creative materials, promoted children's use of mathematical processes to think, create, and construct things that demonstrated their thinking in a dynamic fashion.

The Chicago Art Institute's Lion

In an attempt to revisit the lion study and continue developing and engaging the children's curiosity, the teacher took the children to the Art Institute of Chicago several months after learning about the Reggio Emilia San Prospero Lion. They explored the properties and attributes of the lion statues located at the entrance to the museum and had many discussions about their experiences. In one of the follow-up activities, the teachers provided the children with another lion photograph with a similar perspective as the San Prospero Lion photograph. The following presents the children's representations and dialogue.

Figure 3.13. Lion at the Chicago Art Institute

Figure 3.14. The kindergartner's drawing of the lion

Child A: *I notice that the Reggio lion is brown, and the Chicago lion is yellow.*

Child B: *That one is light gray, and this one is a little bit yellow and golden.*

Child A: *And they're both made out of stone. Also, the Reggio lion's mane goes straight down and the Chicago lion has over-lines . . . it's puffy.*

Child B: *The sky is darker there and this moon is littler, because this is a half moon and that is a full moon.*

Child A: *Well, the first lion's face is round and the other lion's face is long.*

Child B: *And this one has a short face.*

Child A: *The Chicago lion must be the older one because he looks like a papa.*

Child B: *And the other lion looks like the mama. The papa lion is thinking he should protect the family from the predators.*

Child A: *I think the lion is trying to find his way home because he got lost. He was chasing predators from Africa to downtown Chicago. He was running a lot and came to the ocean and swam a lot. He's going to try to find his way back. He's looking at the moon to try and find his way home. By looking at the moon he can find his home because the moon goes everywhere, and he knows how to get there.*

Child B: *Yeah, if you go under it and follow the moon, you can find his cave. When he gets there the family is going to ask him if he found food.*

Child A: *Then the lion is going to come back outside and look at the moon and tell it, "Thank you for helping me find my home."*

Child B: *Then he's going to eat dinner with his family.*

Child A: *Then the next day he's going to visit his cousin in Reggio, and together they're going to hunt for gazelles. They are going to have a feast.*

Figure 3.15. Preschooler's Chicago Art Institute lion drawing

Creatively and critically, the two children processed and learned many math concepts through their interactions with the materials. As the children drew and traced the lions, they became aware of the lines, shapes, patterns, and sense of numbers involved in creating their clay models of the lions. The kindergartner often describes the patterns he observes on the lions and the castle, and the preschooler practices his sense of numbers as he counts the lines (fur) of the lion's mane up to the number seventy-two. Math is clearly observed and processed as the children created three-dimensional models with clay. The children used addition, subtraction, division, multiplication, measurement, geometry, and algebra to create the clay models of the lions and their contexts. Their teacher facilitated a higher level of math learning by providing materials that instilled curiosity and inspired creativity.

DISCOVERING THE PHYSICAL PROPERTIES AND ATTRIBUTES OF MATERIALS

> From my experience in teaching, I've observed how important it is to use different types of materials in math to give the child opportunities to express him/herself. The materials offer a variety of learning experiences for each child, which helps them internalize the skills being taught. —**Master Teacher Lourdes Molina**

Exploration with materials can be a fun activity for children. The textures found in clay, paint, wood, materials from nature, and many other creative and constructive materials can instill a sense of wonder. The exploration of the materials itself can inspire mathematical learning as the children use measurement, patterns, texture, and other attributes to play with the material. When children learn about the essence of the materials and their transformational possibilities, they imagine new things and begin to make sense of their environments.

Discovering the physical properties of creative and constructive materials can also be a great opportunity for you to teach key math concepts. Beforehand, explore the materials you plan to provide the children. Then identify and describe the physical-property language (see fig. 3.16) you will use during children's investigations. Once you recognize the teachable concepts found in the materials, you can generate a list of the properties' attributes that define the materials' magnitude (size and dimension) and multitude (number units). By using and modeling the math properties and attributes using magnitude and multitude terms with children during interactions, you can engage students in rich mathematical conversations. You will also promote and develop children's advanced math language and higher-level thinking.

Physical Properties and Attributes of Materials

Physical properties are observable characteristics of substances that can be measured. Attributes are observable characteristics that describe properties or objects.

Math- and Science-Based Physical Properties of Materials (Magnitude/Substance)

Length	Strength	Plasticity	Mass	Polarity
Width	Elasticity	Texture	Pressure	Cohesion
Height	Stiffness	Firmness	Momentum	Adhesion
Area	Density	Capacity	Velocity	Temperature
Volume	Stress	Permeability	Speed	Moisture

Figure 3.16.

Math- and Science-Based Physical Attributes

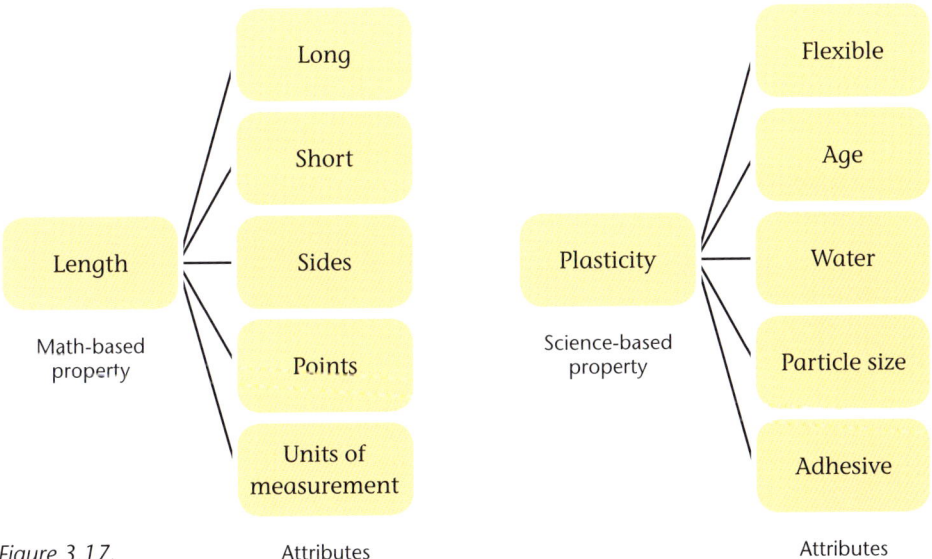

Figure 3.17.

During explorations, it is suggested that teachers allow specific times for children to explore and not interfere with children's play with the materials (Wellhousen and Kieff 2001). Through uninterrupted exploratory play with materials, children learn about the properties (plasticity, permeability, length, weight) and attributes (long, short, wet, dry) of the materials, and eventually use this knowledge to create compositions.

Teachers at the Carole Robertson Center for Learning in Chicago provided the following learning experiences with clay to infant, toddler, and preschool children. By engaging children with this mathematically rich material (clay) throughout their early childhood, teachers can ensure students develop knowledge of the clay's properties and attributes. The mathematical knowledge acquired through these experiences will be useful to the children when they interact with those same concepts in the elementary grades. Look at the children's explorations with clay and think of the mathematizing possibilities that you could provide, as well as the kinds of materials you could add to extend the children's learning.

The children's explorations with clay demonstrate fundamental learning that can occur from infancy through preschool. Beyond the mathematical and scientific learning processing that children experienced when they were provided with rich materials and the time for exploratory play, the students also learned of the transformational possibilities of materials. They began to understand that a material's substance can be manipulated to create real objects and that by engaging in the creative process they can become confident and proficient in their abilities to use materials to develop and communicate ideas, thoughts, and interests. The things they created with clay helped them make sense of the world around them, thereby supporting the multiple facets of learning and development that is important to establish early in life.

Figure 3.18 and *Figure 3.19.* Infants and toddlers exploring clay

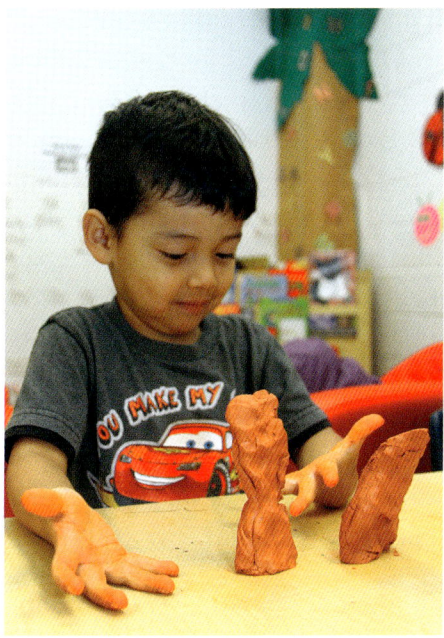 

Figure 3.20 and *Figure 3.21*. Preschoolers exploring the properties and attributes of clay.

CREATE, REPRESENT, AND ROLE-PLAY TO DEVELOP MULTIDIMENSIONAL THINKING SKILLS

The processes of creating, representing, and role playing have similar yet unique characteristics that make them important elements in children's learning. During children's exploration with materials, there may be times when they focus on structure (parts and arrangement in a substance), or they may simply want to experience the enjoyment of creating things. For instance, while I conducted an observation in a preschool classroom, a four-year-old boy began to play with clay for about five minutes. As he rolled the clay back and forth, he looked at me with a joyful expression and said, "This is a worm . . . now it's the letter *L* for my name . . . now it's a heart . . . now I made a car . . ." For the rest of the time, he continued to transform a piece of clay into different things and seemed happy at the process of creating art.

Representations, on the other hand, are children's works of art (concrete) that signify the thinking, experiences, or feelings (abstract) the students are processing at the moment. For example, on one occasion, a five-year-old boy drew a picture of his family going to a restaurant for a birthday celebration. In the picture, his family was sitting at a table with lots of food. All the members of his family were drawn holding hands and with happy faces. This picture represented one of the boy's family traditions that they had just celebrated the week before. The student's representation was a form of communication that described an important occasion in the young boy's life. In it, he represented the experience he shared with others and the emotions that developed through the celebration. The visual detail that he added in the picture lets us know the kinds of thinking he was processing during this activity. The overall learning experience in representational work can be beneficial for children as it provides them a means to express themselves in many ways.

Role playing is also an essential learning strategy that helps students make sense of their daily experiences. As children assume the roles of characters, they begin to analyze and understand the situations that these characters have to deal with, and they learn to see how things function in real life. A good example occurred during a classroom visit where I was observing block play. A four-year-old girl created a beauty salon by building a perimeter with large hollow blocks and using other blocks as chairs. She invited one of the teachers to the salon and engaged in a pretend manicure session. The young girl asked the teacher whether the nails were the right size and if she wanted her to add glitter on top of the nails. After the manicure session was over, the child grabbed a small piece of paper, wrote down some figures, and provided the teacher with an invoice. This role-playing example demonstrates the amount of problem solving that had to take place in order for the play to be successful. This little girl not only created a detailed structure but also was able to manage a thriving business.

The critical and mathematical thinking that develops from creating, representing, and role playing with creative and constructive materials is phenomenal. "Children are innately receptive to the possibilities that materials offer and interact with them to make meaning and relationships, explore, and communicate" (Gandini et al. 2005, 17). In the process of exploring the essence of materials, children become self-guided learners. They also develop an understanding of and learn to play constructively with materials. Students also learn to communicate and express their ideas through the transformation of materials.

In multidimensional thinking, creative thinking involves

- generating new ideas;
- seeking out solutions to a problem;
- making associations among the content presented without prior experience; and
- searching for an answer.

Critical thinking, on the other end of the spectrum, involves processes such as

- separating a whole into parts in order to understand its composition;
- seeking out the probability of a situation and the search for a single solution;
- following a step-by-step process; and
- searching for the answer.

Mathematical processing involves both creative and critical thinking, as individuals use math to quantify and construct meaning of their experiences in life. Representational work with materials can support children's higher-level thinking, as the materials teachers provide strongly influence the quality of the students' learning and thinking. With this in mind, purposeful teachers can plan for the thinking the children will process along with the content the students will be learning during a study or unit lesson.

In the mathematizing process while working with materials, one of the best teaching strategies is to allow children to experience the architectural process of planning, designing, and constructing. The science and art of architecture provides early childhood teachers with wonderful fodder for planning and implementing lessons using creative and constructive materials. A great example of how teachers can promote children's creative, critical, and mathematical thinking through materials occurs in the following learning experiences provided to students from Master Teacher David Banzer. Follow two of the children's projects that occurred during a monthlong study.

Bridge Study and Project

The children became interested in learning about bridges, so David Banzer created a long-term bridge study as part of his mathematical physics in urban engineering project. In an effort to help the children learn about the structure and function of bridges, the teacher brought various materials for the children to create structures and different tools to encourage problem solving. The children first created blueprints to portray different designs for their bridges. Then they explored the physical properties and attributes of the materials. Within the exploration of materials discussion, the small group identified and described properties such as length, width, height, flexibility, tension, plasticity, hardness, and weight.

Figure 3.23. Children exploring the math properties of materials

Figure 3.22. Teacher and children discussing their blueprints

Figure 3.24. Children sharing their bridge designs with materials

Figure 3.25. Children's first bridge construction

The students proceeded to take turns designing bridges with the various materials and collaborating on creating final constructions based on their sharing of ideas. Challenges related to tension and compression resulted. The children tried different solutions to connect the decks, towers, anchorages, and cables together, but nothing worked. Banzer challenged the children by encouraging them to test different kinds of connecting materials to find a solution. In the end, the winning material was clay, as a child reasoned that the clay, once hardened, would sustain the tension placed on the cable.

In two days of work, the students used creative and constructive materials in a cognitively demanding and rigorous process. They drew blueprints of the bridges with different media, explored the properties and attributes of the materials, shared design ideas for each construction, worked together on the construction of the chosen designs, and constructed multiple bridges with the materials. In each of the two days, Banzer mathematized the concepts of length, height, angles, number and operations, weight, and patterns, based on the interests of the children. He provided the materials, language, and inquiry necessary for children to make sense of the math in their context. He facilitated the children's collaboration in a respectful and purposeful manner. The children continued their bridge study for many weeks, acquiring knowledge and developing perspectives throughout their experiences with the materials and with each other.

Figure 3.26. Teacher and children looking at pictures of bridges

Figure 3.27. Children exploring the math properties of materials

Figure 3.28. Children using materials to share their bridge designs

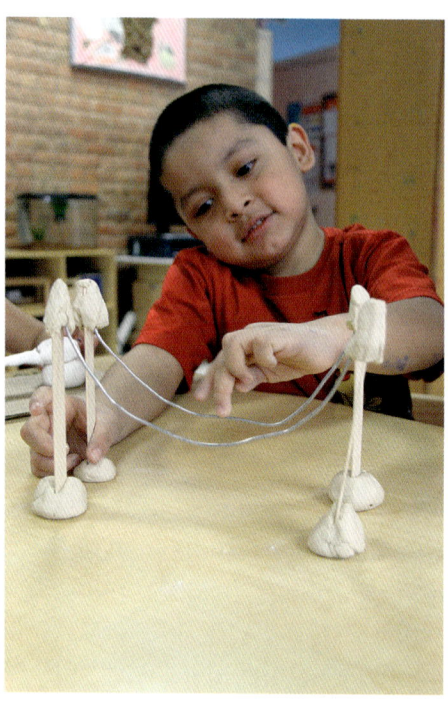

Figure 3.29. Children presenting the final bridge construction

4

Language Modeling Component

Modeling language is essential for teachers working in early childhood settings, as young children are beginning to listen to and acquire verbal language. Incorporating language strategies and techniques is also important for English-language learners as they seek to develop extensive social and academic language so they can actively participate in deep conversations with adults and their peers. Most importantly, language modeling is critical in any early childhood classroom, as teachers need to supplement and compensate for the language children hear or do not hear at home.

Research about language and math learning at the early childhood level tells us that, generally, low-income level children's mathematical performance may be less proficient than their middle-income children counterparts (Ginsburg et al. 2008, 5). The research indicated that this occurs because low-income level children do not receive the mathematical experiences at home needed to develop strong math language and inquiry skills. When a strong mathematical foundation is not developed at home, children may have difficulty engaging in math conversations and discussions within formal school settings. The research about the kinds of math learning that is provided to students tells us that there is "a paucity of higher-level mathematical concepts" (Rudd et al. 2008, 5). This means that oftentimes teachers may incorporate math learning that focuses only on the lower-level mathematical concepts, such as labeling and counting numbers, and spatial awareness. Higher-level math, which includes patterns (algebra), operations (addition, subtraction), and data analysis (graphs and charts) may be provided less often. Furthermore, "language is the primary medium of learning and knowledge" (Eide and Eide 2006, 148–49). Therefore it is important that teachers develop their abilities to engage children in rich math conversations so that students can learn to communicate mathematically within different educational settings.

These research insights relay very important messages about the opportunity and the need for developing children's verbal, expressive, and cognitive math processing and learning. Low-income level children need high-quality interactions and language modeling to acquire the strong verbal and expressive language skills that will help them perform at the same level as their classmates. Teachers can increase a child's ability to understand and apply mathematics. This can be accomplished by integrating higher-level thinking math concepts and language into the student's classroom experiences. Teachers should look beyond implementing simple math processing activities found in commercialized manipulatives that focus on targeted concepts in isolation. Teachers would do well to create and implement high-level mathematical thinking experiences through creative and constructive materials. Teachers also need to be able to verbalize the math concepts and learning with their students, their peers, and the school community.

DEVELOPING MATH GRAMMAR

Children's language and conversation skills are fundamental for future academic success. However, the number of math words and the quality of the mathematical conversations between teachers and children has to be exceptional, especially for low-income/low-resource children who "may have insufficient experience with adult generated language that can help them organize mathematical experience" (Ginsburg 2010). Teachers need to become proficient in the language and grammar of mathematics and be able to help children use and understand math vocabulary. "Such opportunities to build important mathematical vocabulary and concepts abound in any classroom, and the alert teacher takes full advantage of them" (NAEYC 2010, 7).

Teachers can learn to develop children's mathematical vocabulary by promoting the awareness and understanding of math language and grammar. "There is no doubt that one's understanding of language is hugely enhanced by a knowledge of basic grammar. . . . The importance of mathematical grammar is that the statements of mathematics are supposed to be precise" (Gowers et al. 2008, 8). Through teachers modeling precise math language to children during daily interactions in the classroom, the probability of children acquiring and using advanced math language and concepts becomes greater.

Like linguistic grammar, math grammar is the study and acquisition of math words and symbols found within environments. The grammar of mathematics includes words found in the National Council of Teachers of Mathematics math standards (number sense, measurement, algebra, geometry, and data analysis) (NCTM 2000); parts of speech (nouns, adjectives, verbs); and in topics and concepts such as physical properties, structure, function, cognition, expressions, generalizations, and many other areas and processes. Math grammar in this perspective encompasses all the language mechanisms and information needed to make sense of mathematics within any specific context.

Understanding and implementing math grammar and concepts in the classroom help teachers and children develop the ability to analyze data, recognize patterns, and reason logically. Researchers developed the following math word lists to help teachers organize and become aware of the various uses and contexts of math grammar.

Math Content Words

Number and Operations

- addition
- after
- all gone
- altogether
- amount
- backward
- before
- count
- difference
- different from
- division
- equal
- estimate
- fewer
- first
- forward
- groups
- how many
- last
- least
- less
- less than
- minus
- more
- more than
- most
- multiplication
- next
- numbers
- one-half
- one-quarter
- one-third
- pairs
- plus
- sequence
- sets
- subtraction
- sum
- take away
- tally
- the same as
- zero

Measurement

- area
- around
- centimeter
- decrease
- degree
- distance
- Fahrenheit
- far
- feet
- heavy
- high
- holds
- hour
- inches
- increase
- length
- less
- light
- low
- measure
- meter
- minute
- more
- narrow
- near
- second
- short
- start
- tall
- time
- volume
- weight
- wide
- yards

Algebra

- acceleration
- arrange
- classify
- combination
- compare
- constant
- decline
- diagonal
- different
- equal
- fractions
- gravity
- group
- halves
- horizontal
- incline
- match
- order
- parts
- patterns
- place
- same
- sequence
- set
- similar
- slope
- solution
- solve
- sort
- speed
- steep
- velocity
- vertical

Geometry

- angle
- circle
- cone
- corner
- cube
- curve
- cylinder
- diamond
- direction
- edge
- end point
- face
- flat
- hexagon
- line
- oval
- point
- rectangle
- round
- side
- sphere
- square
- start point
- straight
- symmetry
- trapezoid
- triangle

Data Analysis

- always
- amount
- analyze
- attribute
- between
- chart
- collect
- compare
- data
- fewer than
- gather
- graph
- lines
- more than
- never
- organize
- predict
- represent
- sometimes
- sort
- tally

Math Nouns

Math nouns can be physical things such as structures and objects as well as abstract concepts such as quantity, numbers, space, and expressions with numbers.

Concrete Nouns (Countable Common Nouns)

- abacus
- blocks
- building
- calculator
- calendar
- cards
- cash register
- castle
- clay
- clock
- cone
- cube

- cups
- cylinder
- dominoes
- door
- engine
- geometric solids
- house
- links
- measuring tape
- music
- pencil
- photograph
- plate
- prism
- protractor
- pyramid
- ruler
- scale
- sphere
- structure
- tally counter
- thermometer
- timer
- tools
- tower
- wheels
- wire

Abstract Nouns

- addition
- age
- autumn
- border
- chart
- collection
- columns
- data analysis
- depth
- design
- dimension
- direction
- distance
- division
- form
- height
- layout
- length
- lines
- measurement
- multiplication
- numbers
- numerals
- objects
- parallel
- patterns
- perpendicular
- pictures
- plane
- rows
- sequence
- shape
- side
- size
- speed
- subtraction
- surface
- symmetry
- time

Math Adjectives

Math adjectives describe concrete/abstract math nouns and provide the analyzing language needed to begin examining, investigating, and evaluating the patterns in people, places, and things.

Numeral Adjectives

Cardinal numeral adjectives: one, two, three, . . . ten, . . . fifty, . . . one hundred, . . . one thousand

Ordinal numeral adjectives: first, second, third, . . . tenth, . . . fiftieth, . . . one hundredth, . . . one thousandth

Shape Adjectives

- broad
- chubby
- circular
- conical
- crooked
- cubical
- curved
- cylindrical
- deep
- diagonal
- diamond-shaped
- distorted
- elastic
- flat
- hollow
- horizontal
- narrow
- oval
- round

- shallow
- skinny
- spherical
- square
- squiggly
- steep
- straight
- triangular
- twisted
- vertical
- wavy
- zigzag

Size Adjectives

- average
- big
- colossal
- enormous
- extended
- giant
- gigantic
- great
- hefty
- high
- huge
- immense
- jumbo
- large
- little
- low
- mammoth
- massive
- medium
- miniature
- petite
- short
- slender
- slim
- small
- tall
- teeny
- thin
- tiny
- trim
- weighty
- wide

Time Adjectives

- ancient
- brief
- early
- fast
- first
- future
- hasty
- last
- late
- long
- modern
- new
- old
- overdue
- past
- present
- punctual
- quick
- rapid
- short
- slow
- swift
- tardy
- young

Temperature Adjectives

- boiling
- burning
- breezy
- chilly
- cold
- cool
- damp
- dry
- freezing
- frigid
- frosty
- hot
- humid
- icy
- lukewarm
- melted
- mild
- nippy
- scorching
- sizzling
- steaming
- temperate
- warm
- wet

Quantity Adjectives

- abundant
- all
- a lot
- another
- any
- each
- empty
- enough
- equal
- every
- extra
- few
- full
- greater
- half
- heavy
- least
- less
- light
- little

- many
- more
- most
- much
- multiple
- no
- numerous
- once
- only
- plenty
- same
- several
- some
- substantial
- whole

Math Verbs

Math verbs convey actions/movement and are fundamental in thinking intuitively and abstractly, and in the process of understanding the purpose and functions of people, places, and things.

- calculate
- change
- choose
- classify
- compare
- compute
- conclude
- construct
- convert
- count
- create
- decide
- demonstrate
- derive
- describe
- develop
- diagram
- distinguish
- document
- draw
- estimate
- evaluate
- follow directions
- formulate
- generate
- graph
- group
- identify
- interpret
- manipulate
- measure
- memorize
- operate
- order
- plan
- point
- practice
- predict
- propose
- prove
- recognize
- reproduce
- separate
- show
- simplify
- solve
- sort
- state
- tabulate
- tell
- validate

Math Adverbs

Like adjectives, adverbs are describing words. However, adverbs describe verbs whereas adjectives describe nouns or pronouns. Adverbs tell *how*, *when*, or *where* an action takes place.

How

- altogether
- approximately
- evenly
- higher
- highest
- lower
- lowest
- quicker
- quickest
- quickly
- rapidly
- slower
- slowest
- slowly
- speedily
- swiftly

When

- after
- already
- always
- annually
- before
- daily
- during
- last
- later
- monthly
- never
- now
- often
- recently
- soon
- today
- tomorrow
- usually
- weekly
- yesterday

Where

- above
- around
- away
- backward
- behind
- below
- beneath
- beside
- between
- bottom
- closer
- everywhere
- far
- farther
- forward
- here
- in front
- inside
- left
- near
- outside
- over
- right
- there
- through
- top
- under

Math Prepositions/Conjunctions

Prepositions indicate relationships between nouns and other words in sentences. Conjunctions are words that connect words, phrases, and sentences. Knowledge of prepositions and conjunctions is needed for working with math expressions and operations.

- above
- across
- after
- along
- also
- and
- around
- as well as
- at
- atop
- before
- behind
- below
- beneath
- beside
- between
- beyond
- both
- but
- by
- close to
- down
- during
- either
- far from
- following
- for
- from
- in front of
- inside
- into
- left of
- like
- minus
- near
- near to
- next
- next to
- not
- of
- on
- once
- onto
- on top of
- opposite
- or
- out
- outside
- over
- plus
- right of
- round
- so
- than
- throughout
- to
- toward
- under
- underneath
- up
- within
- without

Other Math Concepts

Money/Business

- acquisition
- amount
- bank
- bills
- cash
- change
- charge
- check
- coin
- cost
- credit
- currency
- date
- debt
- dime
- dollar
- donate
- earn
- funding
- item
- money
- nickel
- pay
- payment
- penny
- poverty
- purchase
- quantity
- quarter
- salary
- sale
- save
- sell
- spend
- subtotal
- tax
- total
- wages
- wealth

Math grammar is composed of these and many other words, which together create an extensive collection. When teachers intentionally use math grammar in their daily conversations with students, the quality of children's language and thinking increases. Because of the importance of developing students' academic language, it is critical that teachers begin to assess their own math language and grammar usage. This can be accomplished by recording the conversations teachers are having with children during play. Once teachers evaluate and reflect upon their conversations with students, they can plan to develop their math grammar and use language-modeling techniques. This helps to scaffold and engage children in meaningful learning experiences.

The following language-modeling components are important strategies and techniques that teachers can incorporate in their classrooms to help children develop a strong foundation in verbal and expressive mathematics.

- labeling language
- expanding and extending language
- parallel talk

Figure 4.1. Family child care teacher Linda Hermes provides rich math language while reading *Mouse Count* to children.

- spiral talk
- high frequency math words
- math word family collaboration
- math content, reasoning, and proof charts
- engaging in ongoing, sustained, and in-depth conversations

LABELING LANGUAGE

Labeling language is the first language-modeling technique you can implement with young children in the Mathematizing for Learning Process. This entails you describing and labeling or naming the nouns (objects/elements/entities/things) that the children are observing and interacting with, such as "ball," "tree," "truck," "square." You can label many of the objects children have become interested in until the children are able to name the objects on their own. As children become more proficient at naming objects, you can promote further language development by adding adjectives (descriptive math words) to the labels, such as "round ball," "tall tree," "long truck," "big square." This process helps children construct phrases and helps them first learn math language.

EXPANDING AND EXTENDING LANGUAGE

You can use the next two language techniques to develop children's conversational language skills by *expanding* and *extending* student's speech. When a child states a simple phrase such as, "Ball go," you could restate and complete the sentence, "The ball is going" as a form of expanding the child's response. You could also extend the same phrase by adding more-sophisticated math words, which adds to the complexity of the sentence: "The ball is going fast across the gym floor."

These two language techniques are very important for young children. They help children listen to and make sense of the sound patterns in speech. Expanding and extending language promotes children's syntax development. They learn that multiple sounds uttered in sequence can be used as a form of communication. This syntactic development in infants and toddlers is noticeable when they enter the babbling stage of language acquisition. As toddlers begin to combine consonant and vowel sounds (baba, mama, dada), the children exposed to rich-language-modeling adults will develop conversational babbling. The length of the babbling sounds they produce matches the length of the adult's speech. If children are not exposed to intentional verbal exchanges with adults, it may take longer for them to move from the one-word stage into the phrase and sentence stages. Opportunities to expand and extend children's language occur on a daily basis, so it is beneficial for you to be prepared to elaborate children's speech and conversations when the moment presents itself.

PARALLEL TALK

Parallel talk is the fourth technique you can incorporate in the classroom. It involves having you describe or map children's actions with language. Alice Honig states that in parallel talk "Your words describe what is going on, what children are doing and feeling" (Honig 1999, 5). Parallel talking is an effective language-modeling technique that you can use with children during work and play. It not only models and teaches children language, but it also establishes a respectful learning relationship and child-centered approach. By using this technique, you are providing the children with the language of the concepts and ideas they are interested in investigating.

Figure 4.2. There are many opportunities to use parallel talk with children in a classroom.

You can parallel talk with simple phrases, such as "You are dancing" and "You are stacking." Or you could describe children's actions with more detail: "You are dancing side to side to the music!" and "You are stacking all the blocks up very high!" In other instances, you can use more-sophisticated words as you parallel talk: "You are pushing the large truck across the floor with so much force!" and "Look at how fast the car accelerates as it travels down the ramp!" By listening to advanced math language and engaging in experiences that make those words come to life, children learn complex words and how to use them. They acquire the ability to use the words within their environments.

SPIRAL TALK

A fifth powerful and very effective language-modeling technique is called *spiral talking*. You repeat a targeted word or words ten to twenty times within the context of what a child is doing. This technique was created to help teachers focus and incorporate intentional academic language during their conversations with children. "You're *adding* blocks to the tall structure. How many more blocks are you going to *add*? You're going to *add* five more blocks to your tall structure? Let's see what happens when you *add* the five blocks. Why did the tower fall when you *added* the fifth block? How else can you position the five blocks so they won't fall when you *add* them on top of each other? Look at the positioning of the third block you *added*. Do you think it is positioned well to hold the next block you are going to *add*? Okay, *add* the next block and let's see the outcome. It worked! You *added* all the blocks on top of each other and the structure did not fall!" The language-spiraling pattern continues throughout the interaction, and the key words are sustained or shifted based on the children's mathematical interests.

> The spiral talk technique was extremely effective in my work with children because it helped me to focus in on what mathematical concept the child was really interested in exploring. Children's language developed, their utterances increased in length and complexity, and their cognitive abilities also grew so that they could answer questions and engage verbally with me. —**Master Teacher Sarah Collentine**

Spiral talking allows you to intentionally teach key math words and concepts that children would not otherwise acquire independently through play. The quality of the language modeled through spiral talk has a direct impact on how a child's complex, high-level, and sophisticated vocabulary develops. Holly Lane and Stephanie Allen state, "By modeling the use of sophisticated words, teachers can promote student's vocabulary growth and word consciousness" (Lane and Allen 2010, 1). While refraining from directing children's focal points, you can provide students with the language that aligns with the actions and concepts they have chosen to investigate. This statement rings true in many contexts as often adults want to lead children's thoughts and processing without the child's consent.

Traditionally, in a teacher-directed classroom environment, adults lead students' thoughts and interfere with their learning processing when they observe children creating objects. Teachers may tell them *what* they have created (bypassing the children's interests). These teachers either model or explain *how* children should develop the structure further (interfering with the children's thinking and problem solving). When you want to know *what* the children are creating, allow the children to describe their own creations. If the students have limited language skills, then you can parallel or spiral talk by describing children's actions and creations with enthusiasm: "I see you adding blocks to your tall structure. It's four levels high!" or "Look at all the lines on your drawing! I see some long, curved lines and some short, zigzag lines."

Spiral Talk

Figure 4.3.

By describing their actions and creations, you provide the children with prompts that help them think about and respond to what they are doing and what they have created. Your role is to facilitate learning by providing objective language and feedback. As for the *how* of what children are creating, you can continue language modeling. Begin to ask open-ended questions to help children think critically about what they have chosen to create and represent with materials. The use of child-centered language-modeling techniques can help support children's language development organically through respectful and purposeful interactions.

In the following vignette, preschool teacher David Banzer uses multiple language-modeling techniques, with an emphasis on math language, to engage and provide children with vocabulary to describe what they are experiencing and thinking at the block area. The conversation was recorded digitally, transcribed, and then graphed to capture the quantity and quality of math language the teacher provided his students. Part of the teacher's language is provided in the following transcription.

David Banzer language modeling with a small group of preschool children in the block area:

You're going to add those blocks on top?

Are you going to make it taller? Are you going to make the walls taller, or are you going to stop there?

You want to make it taller? Okay.

So you're going to add another block on top?

And you're adding some triangles on top right there.

Are you going to add another block on top? And make it taller?

So I see three blocks on top of each other now . . . and then the triangles on top.

You're lining up at the ends?

Triangles on top of those.

They fell over? They fell down?

You don't think you should put the triangles on the top yet? On the walls . . .

You're still adding blocks on top to make the walls taller.

Do you want to add more blocks to make them taller too? Because you're adding the triangles on top of them, right? On top of the walls.

Yeah, you could take those away.

Do you think you should take those off? You could take those away and then put some . . . you're going to put . . . oh just one triangle on top? Okay.

When you took . . . ah, you took them away and now you're putting them together to make . . .

Putting the triangles together to make a bigger triangle.

So you put triangles together in a pattern and you put them . . . and now you're going to put them away?

No? Are you going to put them back . . . oh, I think you want to build it taller.

So you're still adding more. Are you ready to add your triangle?

Will you use the four triangles to make a bigger triangle? You want to add that on top now?

And you're going to add more blocks on . . .

Are you going to make the walls the same height, the same . . . ?

When they go up . . . So there's three blocks going up on their sides on that way.

You want to add more over here?

And you keep adding blocks . . . and you're taking the triangles away, and then putting them up another level . . . of blocks.

So I see four now. And you're going to add your triangles on top of that?

And you're going to add some more on the long side? Yeah.

So you're still adding the triangles to the top of that wall? Yeah.

Every time she adds more you have to take those away though.

Now we're getting really tall. Remember how it was short to begin with, and you guys said, "we're going to put stuff in the middle of the house"? Now it looks like you want to add more on top to make it bigger. Make it taller.

So, this wall is really tall. I see one, two, three, four, five blocks on top of each other. On that side it's shorter isn't it?

Are you going to add more blocks to that side?

Yep, are you going to add? Are you going to go around the long wall first before you get to the short wall? Yeah.

Are you just going to work on those triangles over there?

Ah, okay, how many do you have?

So you're going to make it tall . . . are you going to make the triangle taller and bigger?

The significance of the language modeling in this ten-minute interaction is fundamental as the teacher clearly planned to mathematize children's actions with an abundance of math language (see fig. 4.4). Imagine a teacher that mathematizes and language models math language at the block area every day for the whole school year. Even greater, imagine a teacher mathematizing and language modeling in the block area for ten minutes, at the house area for another ten minutes, and so forth throughout all the classroom interactions, activities, and routines. The outcome for children would be an enriched language experience that provides them with the necessary verbal knowledge and skills to help them make sense of the things they are investigating.

Math Language Graph

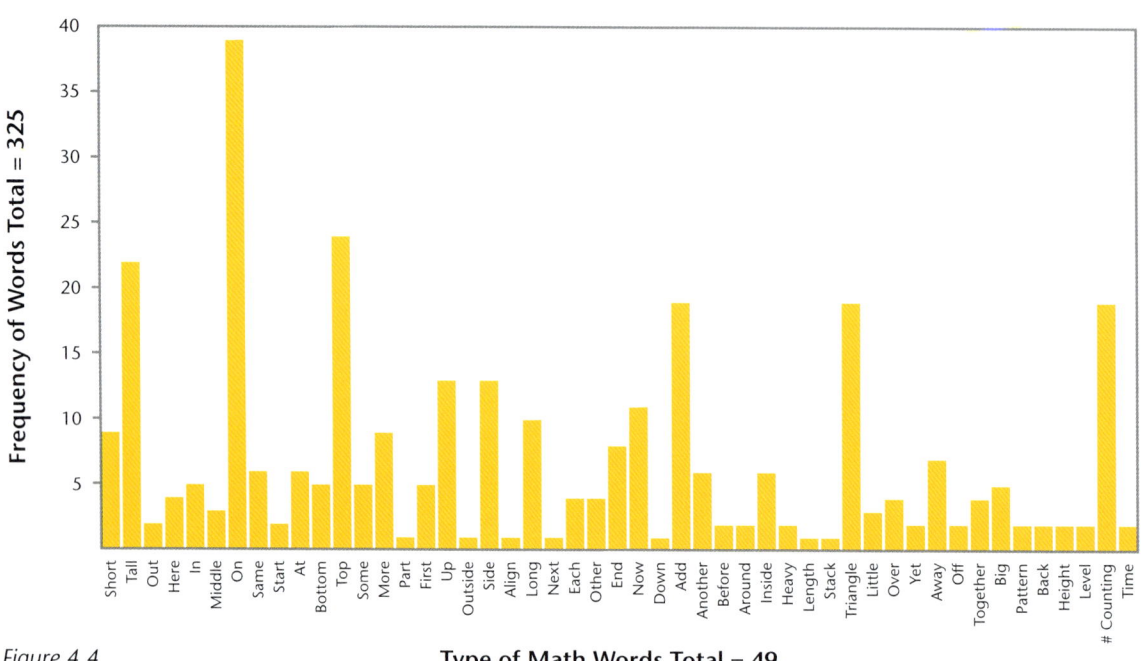

Figure 4.4.

80,000 MATH WORD DIFFERENCE

Quantifying teacher's math language and utilizing the data to inform professional-development efforts has been a project I have undertaken in many educational contexts. The quantity and quality of teacher math-language modeling in the classroom varies at different schools, but the implications are critical. Math-language samples collected from more than sixty preschool teachers suggest that there is a huge range of the type and frequency of math language modeled to students. During the collection period, there was a 310-math-word-exposure difference between the highest-scoring teacher and the lowest (325 – 15 = 310 words [see below]). If we extrapolate the results in this case, there could be a 76,880-math-word difference between the math language provided by a proficient mathematizing teacher and a novice teacher, if both are interacting with children for ten minutes a day, over an entire school year.

Teacher #1 total math words = 325 (10 min.) (325 × 248 school days = 80,600)
Teacher #2 total math words = 15 (10 min.) (15 × 248 school days = 3,720)
Difference: 80,600 – 3,720 = 76,880 (80,000 rounded number) math words

Though the yearly number is extrapolated, the reality is that unless teachers are trained, coached, and supported with extensive math content and processing knowledge, skills, and dispositions, the amount of rich math language exposure to students can be limited and the learning gap extensive.

As a result of my work with teachers during professional learning communities, I created the following three instructional charts to support teachers in the process of

- increasing their math vocabulary,
- developing language-modeling skills, and
- understanding the kinds of mathematical learning that can occur within all the classroom areas.

HIGH-FREQUENCY MATH WORDS CHARTS

In an effort to help you incorporate key math words and engage children in great mathematical conversations in all the interest areas, create and display high-frequency math words charts in different areas of a classroom. Below is a sample chart of high-frequency math words you can post as you are mastering the math language and grammar used during conversations with students at the water table.

High-Frequency Math Words at the Water Table

Nouns	Adjectives	Verbs	Adverbs	Prepositions/ Conjunctions
Cup	Empty	Pour	Slowly	In
Top	Full	Fill	Quickly	Up
Bottom	More	Add	Inside	Down
A lot	Plus	Count	Outside	Over
Half				

Figure 4.5.

When children engage with "liquid measurement" and "dry measurement" concepts and materials at the water table, you can provide containers that integrate the "cup" unit of measurement. Containers that measure one-half cup, one cup, two cups, and four cups can help children explore the customary unit of measurement for volume. Using these materials, children will begin to develop the understanding of a part-to-whole relationship in that two one-half cups fill one cup, four one-half cups fill two cups, and so forth. You could then follow up by providing the cup unit measurement or capacity/volume language based on children's actions with the materials at the water table. The goal is for you to become proficient in applying the math language in any setting to the point where it becomes instinctual.

MATH WORD FAMILY COLLABORATION CHARTS

When children are investigating a math concept in any classroom interest area, there are specific math words (math family) that work together to help children develop an understanding of that specific math concept. These word families come from the various math strands—number sense, measurement, algebra, geometry. For example, when children are constructing with unit blocks and are explicitly focused on building a tall structure, there are specific math words that aid in the understanding of the concept of height. This height illustration demonstrates how this process works.

Math Word Family Collaboration

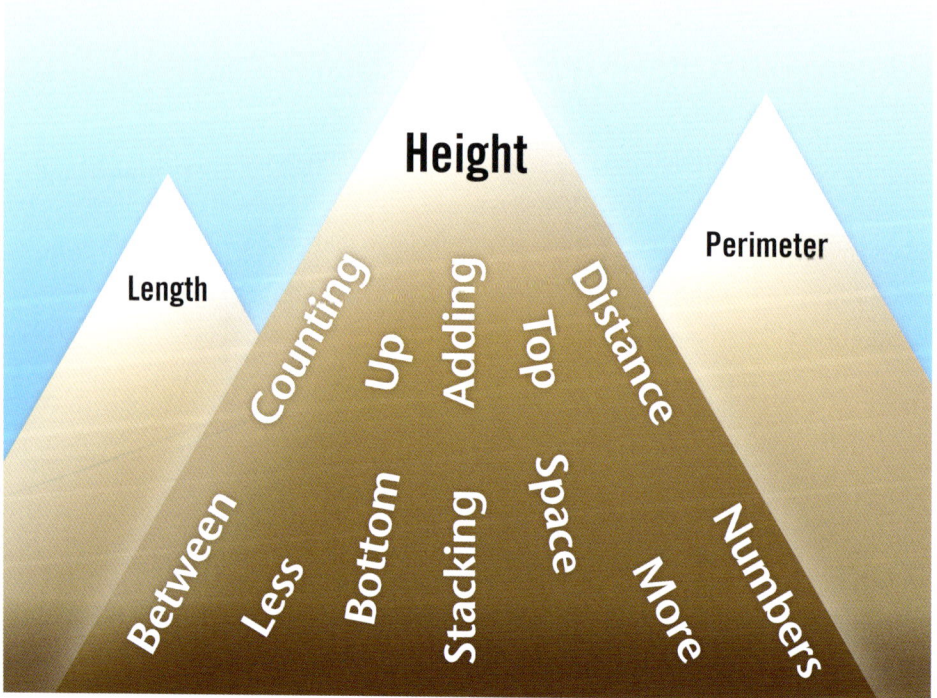

Figure 4.6.

The strategy here is to mathematize by observing and interpreting children's context and content potential, then use the math word family tied to the concept the students are investigating. Every math concept can be developed by finding a specific math word family and providing intentional language modeling and inquiry interactions throughout children's explorations and creative processes.

When you create math word family collaboration illustrations based on the different math concepts that will be investigated in the classroom, you can learn to apply and develop children's math knowledge with more precision.

MATH CONTENT, REASONING, AND PROOF CHARTS

Teaching key vocabulary words is a critical component for the math teacher. Children not only have to be introduced to or taught the content language but also the reasoning and proof math language. One specific example of the importance of teaching math reasoning and proof language occurred during a teacher-coaching visit I made many years ago. The teacher was explaining how he had taught the children the concept of height. The teacher called upon his brightest student, indicated some toy dinosaurs, and asked, "Could you tell Mr. Allen which one is tall and which one is short?" The child pointed to the T. rex and said, "This one is tall and this one [triceratops] is short."

I complimented the child and stated how wonderful it was that she knew which dinosaur was tall and which one was short. However, when I asked her why she thought the T. rex was tall and the triceratops was short, she stated, "The T. rex has feet and the triceratops has horns." Even though the child was able to answer the question through her own interpretation, her response provides a perfect example of how children need multiple experiences to make sense of math concepts. You can support children's understanding by teaching, directly and indirectly, the math content, reasoning, and proof language (language we used to support a statement with evidence) organically in all classroom experiences.

For this child to respond correctly to my question, the teacher would have to provide many engaging experiences for the student to understand that the answer is about height. The child would have to learn the words *tall* and *short* as well as *top, bottom, distance, space, between, more,* and *less* to be able to compare the two objects. The teacher would also have to language model and provide experiences with nonstandard or standard units of measurement in order for the child to understand the proof of the equation. The reason why the T. rex is taller is because the distance between the top of the triceratops to the top of the T. rex is five inches, therefore the T. rex is five inches taller.

Conceptualizing the meaning of height or any other math concept is a complex task. Children may not be able to provide the literal description. However, given enough time to explore with materials and to interact with teachers who can guide them in math conceptual development, children can learn to explain the concepts with great detail. In order for children to learn mathematical skills effectively, teachers can consider the math content and reasoning language needed to think critically with language. It is important that teachers analyze each math concept to be taught and strategically define both simple and complex math words associated with that topic. Without providing the more complex math vocabulary words within the context of the children's environment, the depth of content can be lost and children could be left with superficial learning.

The following tables demonstrate how you could think about the simple and complex math word possibilities found in any concept before lessons or experiences are incorporated.

Concept: Height

Content Language	Reasoning Language	Proof Language
Tall, Short	Top, Bottom Distance/Space Between More, Less	*Nonstandard:* Cubes, Blocks, Steps, String, Numbers *Standard:* Inches, Feet, Yards, Numbers, Taller, Shorter

Figure 4.7.

Concept: Volume

Content Language	Reasoning Language	Proof Language
Empty, Full	Top, Bottom Space More, Less Same	*Nonstandard:* Containers, Numbers *Standard:* Cups, Ounces, Pints, Gallons, Numbers

Figure 4.8.

The goal of analyzing the math content, reasoning, and proof language being introduced or taught in the classroom is not to expect young children to express themselves accurately, but for you to become explicitly aware of the math language or mathematizing possibilities that can emerge during interactions with children.

ENGAGING IN ONGOING, SUSTAINED, AND IN-DEPTH CONVERSATIONS

Engaging in ongoing, sustained, and in-depth mathematical conversations with children is one of the major goals of the Mathematizing for Learning Process approach. Using precise content knowledge and language techniques, the teacher

- encourages conversations throughout the day,
- engages children in sustained dialogue based on children's interests, and
- develops the concepts the children have focused on.

When you engage in meaningful and purposeful conversations with children, you help support students' language and verbal skills.

Meaningful and Ongoing Conversations

The power and impact of meaningful and ongoing conversations with children has been widely accepted since Betty Hart and Todd Risley's (1995) study found a large discrepancy between the amount of language offered at home to children from professional working families and to children in low-income families during their early years. The data revealed that on average, children from affluent families heard 2,153 words per hour compared to the 616 words provided to children of low-income families. Overall, during children's first three years of life, there was a 30-million-word difference between the two types of families.

Figure 4.9. Master Teacher Matilde Romero mathematizing the concepts of angles, length, and weight during children's marble racer study

The number of words and conversations the children receive from their early childhood teachers also has a great impact on their language abilities and their academic success in later elementary grades. Tim Boals (2001) states that the frequency of social and academic language offered to children throughout the day has a positive or negative impact on children's learning and future academic success. Children are more likely to flourish when teachers engage them in ongoing back-and-forth conversations, showing interest in children's thoughts, ideas, and opinions. This level of engagement occurs when teachers eagerly seek out opportunities to integrate an abundance of math language as they talk with children throughout the day.

Sustained and In-Depth Conversations

The National Association for the Education of Young Children (NAEYC) and the National Council of Teachers of Mathematics (NCTM) published a paper that discussed the topic of sustained and in-depth conversations. In *Early Childhood Mathematics: Promoting Good Beginnings*, the two organizations affirmed the importance of providing "carefully planned experiences that focus children's attention on a particular mathematical idea" (2010, 9). Further, they asserted, "Such concepts can be introduced and explored in large and small group activities and learning centers." The role of mathematical conversations is significant within various group sizes as students can develop language and construct meaning socially via their interactions and interpretations. When you frequently promote sustained and in-depth conversations in various group sizes, children learn to listen, speak, and share their thoughts and ideas in a naturally flowing exchange of information with adults and peers.

A great strategy you can use to assess children's math language acquisition and verbal skills is to capture child interactions on digital recording devices. Through these documentation media, you can observe children's conversations with others and learn what new math words, ideas, and concepts they have mastered or are learning. You can capture students' dialogue and assess whether or not children are thinking in words as they communicate with others or with themselves (self talk). The process of thinking in words is a critical developmental component. It helps children develop knowledge through reasoning, associations, and analogies (Eide and Eide 2006). And it establishes the interrelationship between speech and mental-concept development (Vygotsky 1978).

Kindergartners Math Language while Investigating Measurement Concepts with Various Materials

The following interactions were captured in Erika Yañez's kindergarten classroom as the students investigated different concepts of measurement through various materials, modes of learning, and collaboration. As you follow some of the children's conversations and observe photos of the experiences, identify the math words the children are beginning to learn and use in their experiences, assess the students' verbal skills, and think about the future learning possibilities a teacher can promote based on what happened in these activities.

Student 1: *One, two, three, four, . . . eleven. My shoe is eleven cubes long.*

Student 2: *You're measuring your shoe? Let me measure my shoe. Teacher, this is my shoe. Look how long my shoe is. One, two, three, four, . . . ten. My shoe is ten blocks long and hers is eleven.*

Student 3: *I think hers is thirteen.*

Student 1: *Well hers is ten blocks long and mine is eleven blocks long.*

Student 3: *Let me help you put [on] your shoe.*

Student 2: *Why does it go right here?*

Student 1: *Teacher, where do we write our results?*

Teacher: *You can write your measurement results right here. What sound does this word begin with?*

Student 1: *"B."*

Teacher: *That's right! "B" for book. So the word "book" is in the beginning of your sentence.*

Student 1: *The book . . . is . . . eight inches long (writing on line paper).*

Student 2: *I'm going to measure my book too. One cube, two cubes, three cubes, . . . nine! Nine cubes long! Oh, how do I spell "nine"? Teacher, how do I spell "nine"?*

Teacher: *Good question. Everyone, where can I look to see how to spell "nine"?*

Everyone: *On the number chart!*

Teacher: *That's right, on the number chart! What else are you measuring?*

Student 3: *I have to measure my book.*

Student 4: *Hers is one million cubes long!*

Student 2: *That's way too long.*

Student 3: *Do I need a chalkboard to write on?*

Student 2: *No, you need to do your bar graph on the paper.*

Student 3: *One, two, three, . . . fifteen! Mine is fifteen cubes long.*

Student 2: *Teacher, look at my bar graph.*

Teacher: *What does you bar graph say?*

Student 2: *My bar graph says it's nine cubes long.*

Student 1: *My bar graph is one, two, three, . . . fourteen!*

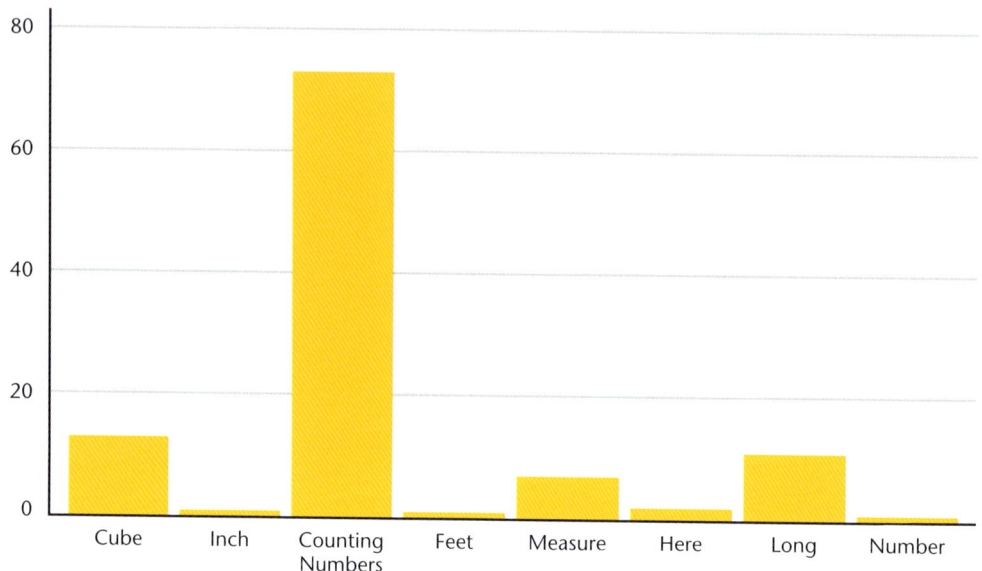

Figure 4.10.

The large and small group interactions regarding a new topic for the classroom were significant for many reasons. First, it allowed the students to learn about the concepts found in measurement through their interests and via the use of various materials. The children used linking cubes to measure books, shoes, and their arms and feet to make sense of the concepts. Second, the teacher guided children in the use of bar graphs (visual) and writing (kinesthetic) as a way to incorporate different modes of learning, and to link mathematics to literacy. Third, the collaboration involved in the experience made the interactions meaningful for children as they continually engaged in conversations to help each other problem solve through the various circumstances. Lastly, the fact that they are using math language to communicate their understanding is a wonderful achievement.

It is obvious from reading the documentation that at different points during the unit lesson, Yañez mathematized, language modeled, and provided the experiences necessary to help children make sense of the topic. Now, a week into the measurement study, the children demonstrate a proficient level of understanding of the various math processes that are needed to measure objects. Based on the conversations, the math language graph, and the photos, you can interpret children's understanding and proficiency levels, and plan more challenging activities, experiences, and routines. This process can help further students' abilities to understand the mathematical relationships that exist within their environments.

Figure 4.11. Exploration of materials

Figure 4.12. Estimating quantity and height

Figure 4.13. Group math-literacy link

Figure 4.14. Data analysis

Figure 4.15. Individual math-literacy link

Figure 4.16. Group mathematical discourse

5

Inquiry Component

The fourth Mathematizing for Learning Process component is inquiry. At this point, the mathematizing teacher has

- observed children and determined the best teaching environment;
- provided great materials for children to explore, problem solve, and create compositions with; and
- modeled sophisticated math language and engaged children in ongoing, sustained, and in-depth conversations.

The teacher is now preparing to develop and challenge children's thinking, based on the activities and conversations they have been experiencing in the classroom.

Inquiry is defined as an "examination into facts or principles" (*Merriam-Webster's Collegiate Dictionary*, 11th ed.). We as early childhood teachers have a responsibility to make the examination of facts and principles, the search for the truth, a great educational experience for children. The Mathematizing for Learning Process approach helps teachers provide children with the concrete (creative/constructive material exploration) and abstract (language/thinking) tools to make their search for the truth successful. The inquiry component takes children to the next level of understanding. It facilitates children's mathematical and multidimensional thinking processes through in-depth discussions and challenges. It creates a culture of reflective practice and establishes collaborative communities in the classroom. It employs quality experiences, sophisticated language modeling, and opportunities to develop multidimensional modes of thinking through inquiry. Through this process, children can become confident, capable learners, ready to engage in the academic challenges they encounter.

HIGHER COGNITIVE PROCESSING

Cognition is defined as "cognitive mental processes," while *thinking* is defined as "the act of using one's mind to produce thoughts" (*Merriam-Webster's Collegiate Dictionary*, 11th ed.). When teachers allow students to use multiple mental processes to make sense of concepts and ideas, children can learn and develop at a higher cognitive level. For this reason, it is important that teachers incorporate learning experiences that intentionally promote holistic thinking and processing. Too often students' thinking becomes one dimensional, as some teachers may teach math skills in strict isolation from the child's environment. An example is the teacher who teaches sequential patterns by making students create color patterns with dinosaur counters. In such cases, students may learn to produce a sequence; however, they may not be able to transfer that knowledge to other contexts. The process of understanding a concept such as patterns works best when it is taught within the many contexts and interests of the children. When rich contexts, multiple perspectives, and multidimensional thinking are not incorporated into the learning process, students' knowledge of any concepts may be based only on memorization. This leaves understanding and learning at a standstill. The following inquiry elements of the Mathematizing for Learning Process approach were created to ensure all children are provided with wonderful opportunities to engage in deeper levels of thinking and learning.

> The most amazing aspect of mathematizing has been the lasting effect on me as a teacher and the subsequent impact on the children. I feel so much more confident in using math language and concepts in my classroom. That comfort has then inspired a classroom full of preschoolers to look at math as a means of problem solving and critical thinking. —**Master Teacher Jennifer Jones**

PROMOTING CREATIVE AND CRITICAL THINKING THROUGH HOLISTIC INTEGRATED PROJECTS

Children can acquire an abundance of mathematical relationships by engaging in activities that stimulate both left- and right-brain processing, and that exercise both creative and critical modes of thinking. In chapter 3, the exploration with materials, the importance of providing open-ended creative and constructive materials for children to explore, play, and create with was proposed. Intentional materials play a significant role in developing children's mental processing configurations. The better the quality of the materials, the better the quality of children's processing and thinking will be. You can strategically promote both modes of thinking by incorporating lesson activities that allow children to process new information in various ways. With this truth in mind, let's take a closer look at the elements and processes of creative and critical thinking, based on theory and research.

Creative thinking can be defined as the process of combining elements with the purpose of forming new structures, functions, or entities (Orlich et al. 2012). Critical thinking can be described as "the art of analyzing and evaluating thinking with a view to improving it" (Paul and Elder 2006), and "the ongoing search for valid and reliable knowledge to guide our beliefs and actions" (Galinsky 2010, 203).

Teachers can strategically implement holistic integrated projects that stimulate both creative and critical thinking. They can also guide children to an awareness of their mathematical thought processing. Through this process, students acquire a deeper level of mathematical knowledge and understanding of the topic at hand. In this holistic approach, children are provided with experiences that challenge them to investigate and examine materials, content, and ideas through different thinking modalities and perspectives. I like to associate the construction of meaning process found in this holistic integrated projects method with the Fibonacci Spiral (see fig. 5.1).

The Fibonacci Spiral is a growing pattern (an increasing sequence used to analyze mathematical changes). It was invented by the most celebrated mathematician of the Middle Ages, Leonardo Pisano Bigollo, who was known as Fibonacci. The connection between the Fibonacci Spiral and the construction of meaning process is as follows: Children are asked to generate ideas about a project (creative thinking, 1) and then are asked to choose one of the ideas and analyze its parts (critical thinking, 1), and are further challenged to produce a new idea (1+1 = 2). As they work through this process, they enter into a continuous spiral of right- and left-brain thinking. As teachers continually promote children's creative and critical thinking, children develop the ability to build on previous thinking and learning (1+2 = 3; 3+2 = 5), making learning a sequential growing pattern. The end goal is to provide children with a systematic approach to thinking that they will continue to use throughout their lives.

The Fibonacci Spiral

Figure 5.1. The Fibonacci Spiral is based on the Fibonacci sequence. In the sequence, each subsequent number is the sum of the previous two: 0, 1, 1, 2, 3, 5, 8, 13, 21, 34, 55, 89, 144 . . .

Holonomy

Holistic integrated projects work well during small-group learning experiences, as they can promote and establish holonomous classroom communities. *Holonomy* is "the notion that an entity is both an autonomous unit and a member of a larger whole simultaneously" (Costa et al. 1999, 1). I define a holonomous community as a group that functions congruently, constructively, and productively within a collaborative learning context. The community functions congruently in the sense that participants engage in a harmonious flow of interests, ideas, and perspectives. They communicate with one another with respect and empathy. The community functions constructively through ongoing learning and development of the group's ideas and processes. There is mutual upbuilding, where all members are accountable for their colleagues' increased development and progress. The community functions productively by producing new valuable ideas, concepts, and creations for the benefit of the group.

HOLISTIC INTEGRATED PROJECT: BRIDGE PROJECT

In this section, Master Teacher Meredith Chambers uses the holistic integrated project approach. She intentionally provides creative and constructive materials for the children to plan, design, and construct a model bridge. The children use both creative- and critical-thinking skills. The children had been involved in a bridge study for a few months as part of Chambers's mathematical physics in urban engineering learning group at the Chinese American Service League Center. The children are concluding their investigation with this final project.

The children began by drawing blueprints of the red bridge they had been visiting for the past month located near their school in Chicago. Students shared their drawings and discussed the mathematical properties of the bridge. These included the bridge's length, width, height, and the patterns found on the railings. Master Teacher Meredith Chambers then provided creative and constructive materials for children to explore. Students analyzed the wood's texture and size by smelling, pressing, squeezing, and following the wood's patterns from both ends with their hands. The small group continued to explore the materials and discussed the math and science physical properties and attributes of the materials. Some of the words and descriptions included *long*, *short*, *diamond patterns*, *cubes*, *rectangles*, *hard*, *flexible*, *soft*, and *rough*. Ms. Chambers continued by asking children challenging questions around the transformational possibilities of the materials.

Figure 5.2. Promoting creative thinking by drawing a blueprint of the red bridge

Figure 5.3. Promoting critical thinking by describing the physical properties of materials

The next part of the project allowed every child to have a turn sharing his or her ideas and designs on how the bridge could be constructed. After the group voted on the preferred design, the children measured, marked, and constructed the base of the bridge with wooden materials. Enthusiastically, one of the children ran to grab some materials and shared the idea that they could use tape to connect the railing to the base. The students agreed and began to attach the railing (ribbon) around the perimeter of the base. They then began to paint the columns, barriers, and railings with red paint to match the color of the neighborhood bridge.

Figure 5.4. Preschool children sharing their bridge designs

Figure 5.5. Measuring their bridge

Figure 5.6. Painting the completed bridge

The final part of this holistic integrated project included a reflective session where children discussed the processes they experienced, challenges they confronted while building the bridge, and the differences and similarities between their structure and the actual bridge. The group of children decided to share their experience with the classroom and presented their bridge to their colleagues during a large-group gathering. The bridge was then put on display at the entrance of the center for the whole school community to observe and enjoy the work and results that the children had achieved through their monthlong bridge study.

Figure 5.7. Proud bridge builders

The teaching strategies and learning goals in the bridge construction projects were for children to

- explore, learn, and understand in-depth mathematical concepts;
- use creative- and critical-thinking skills to help them make meaning of the math they were processing; and
- reflect with teachers and peers on the project before, during, and after the construction, in an effort to develop metacognitive skills (thinking about thinking) and to establish a holonomous community.

Mathematically, students explored and became explicitly aware of the concepts of measurement as children drew and measured their blueprints; measured, marked, and cut the ribbon pieces for the railings; measured and explored the possible designs of the structure; connected the different parts of the bridge; and compared the frame of the structure to their drawings. Students also directly engaged in math learning as they

- measured, counted, and summed the length of the wood pieces;
- added and combined each other's wood pieces to construct the frame of the structure; and
- counted and summed up the length difference between their construction and their drawings.

Further math processing occurred as students used elements of geometry to design and talk about the possible shapes of the bridge. They used language related to math patterns while discussing the diamond shapes on the ribbon. The elaborate mathematical processing and learning of this project embodied how children can learn mathematics constructively.

Cognitively, this project challenged children's minds and immersed them in an ongoing, sustained, and in-depth learning experience. It provided teacher language and inquiry to help them in their quest for truth and learning. The spiraling effect between creative and critical thinking was an innovative method for processing information at a higher cognitive level.

IMPLEMENT HIGH-LEVEL QUESTIONING PATTERNS TO DEVELOP PROBLEM SOLVING, REASONING, AND PROOF SKILLS

Another fundamental element and approach to inquiry that you can integrate is the idea of learning and teaching through the constructivist approach.

Based on child-development theories and research, very young children are intuitive thinkers. They think based on perception (Piaget 1964) and make meaning of knowledge within social contexts (Vygotsky 1978; Bruner 1978). The constructivist teacher values children's ideas, perspectives, processes, pace, and trials and errors. This teacher is extremely patient, knowing that intuitive thinkers at this age are prone to make many mistakes. Therefore, the constructivist teacher follows and nurtures students' paths to the truth of a concept without giving them the answer. Instead, they ask questions that help them find the solution to a problem on their own.

In an effort to help teachers learn about and understand their mathematical questioning patterns during their interactions with children, I created the Questioning Vortex illustration (fig. 5.8) and Questioning Patterns chart (fig. 5.9). These tools showcase the variables of the questioning process. Traditionally, teachers are told to ask open-ended questions without really focusing on any other aspect of the questioning interaction. The illustration and chart promote and guide teachers' analysis of the questioning approaches, content, types, and styles (ACTS) they are implementing with students within specific intervals of time. As teachers complete their own questioning patterns charts, (in this example a ten-minute block-play interaction) and reflect on the four critical aspects of questioning, they become aware of the kinds of interactions they are incorporating in the classroom. With the data collection, they can interpret whether the kinds of questioning patterns, or ACTS, are constructive, productive, and educationally valuable.

Questioning Vortex

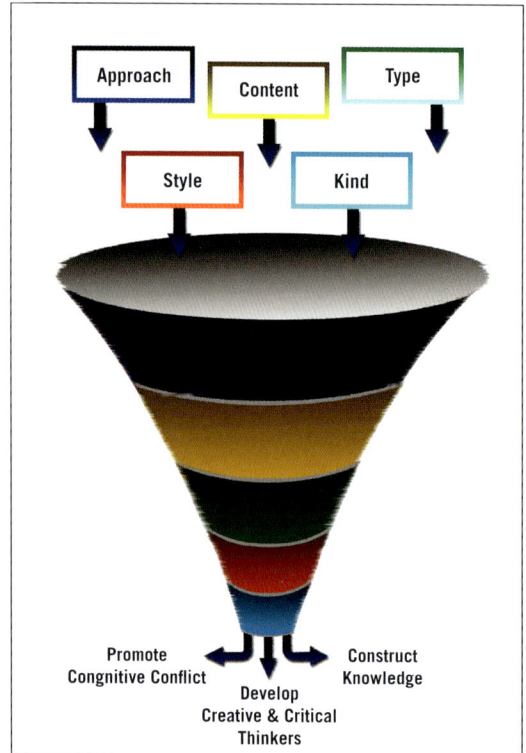

Figure 5.8.

Questioning Approach

One of the first components listed on both the Questioning Vortex illustration and Questioning Patterns chart is the questioning approach. In this process, you analyze each question you ask during an interaction, record each question's approach, and then reflect on the approach patterns that become visible on the questioning approach column. Three essential factors are included in this perspective: the initiation-response-feedback (IRF), funneling, and focusing series.

Questioning Patterns Chart

Number Line (Where question occurred on Transcription)	Questioning Approach (Initiation-Response-Feedback, Funneling, Focusing)	Questioning Content (Numbers & Operations, Geometry, Algebra, Measurement)	Questioning Type (Closed-Ended vs. Open-Ended Responses)	Questioning Style (Attention-Focusing, Quantifying, Spatial Relations, Comparison, Problem-Posing, Reasoning, Proof)
1	IRF	Length Concept	Closed	Attention-Focusing
3	IRF	Length Concept	Open	Attention-Focusing
5	Focusing	Length Concept	Open	Problem-Posing
7	Focusing	Length Concept	Open	Reasoning
10	IRF	Length Concept	Closed	Attention-Focusing
11	Focusing	Length Concept	Open	Proof
12	Funneling	Length Concept	Open	Proof
13	Focusing	Height Concept	Open	Proof
14	Focusing	Height Concept	Open	Reasoning
19	IRF	Other (non-math)	Open	Attention-Focusing
20	Funneling	Height Concept	Open	Problem-Posing
21	Funneling	Height Concept	Closed	Proof
22	Focusing	Height Concept	Open	Reasoning
23	Funneling	Height Concept	Open	Comparison
25	IRF	Height Concept	Closed	Attention-Focusing
27	Focusing	Width Concept	Open	Problem-Posing
29	Focusing	Width Concept	Open	Reasoning
30	Focusing	Width Concept	Open	Reasoning
32	Focusing	Width Concept	Closed	Reasoning
33	Focusing	Perimeter Concept	Open	Comparison
34	IRF	Perimeter Concept	Closed	Attention-Focusing
35	Funneling	Perimeter Concept	Closed	Reasoning
37	IRF	Perimeter Concept	Closed	Attention-Focusing
38	IRF	Number Concept	Closed	Attention-Focusing
40	Funneling	Number Concept	Open	Problem-Posing
51	Funneling	Perimeter Concept	Closed	Comparison
53	IRF	Area Concept	Closed	Attention-Focusing
57	Focusing	Area Concept	Open	Proof
60	Focusing	Area Concept	Open	Quantifying
Etc.	"	"	"	"

Figure 5.9.

Initiation-Response-Feedback (Question or Series of Questions)

This is a teacher-directed approach in which a teacher asks a simple question in order to elicit information from a student. The student responds with a simple answer, and the teacher acknowledges or provides simple feedback. The teacher's level of participation is active, and the student's activity is mainly receptive. The IRF approach can be useful for framing a conversation as it can spark a student's curiosity, attention, or interest.

Example 1:

Teacher: What are you building?

Student: A castle.

Teacher: Oh, you're building a castle!

Example 2:

Teacher: How many blocks do you have?

Student: Three.

Teacher: Yes, you have three blocks.

Funneling (Question or Series of Questions)

Using this teacher-guided approach, the teacher models the learning process or directly coaches the student through the problem-solving experience. The cognitive activity occurs in the adult, and the child responds based on the teacher's thinking. The teacher's level of participation is very active, and the student's activity is either mainly receptive or fairly equally active. This approach is effective when a child cannot comprehend or explain the cognitive or linguistic processing needed to solve a problem. Funneling can be associated with the constructivist theory of teaching.

Examples:

How can we construct a castle twenty-two inches high with the unit blocks?

What would happen if we added eight more blocks vertically to the side of the castle?

Can we look for any alignment problems in your house's foundation?

When we compare the perimeter of our structure with the photo of the castle, what differences and similarities do you see?

Focusing (Question or Series of Questions)

This is a child-centered approach. The adult listens to the student's responses and follows the child's thinking and perspectives, whether correct or incorrect. The cognitive activity occurs in the student, and the adult takes on a facilitator role. The teacher's level of participation is either mainly receptive or equally active, and the student's participation is very active. Focusing values the student's thinking and encourages the student to contribute in the classroom. It is an effective process that increases students' ability to critically reflect, self-regulate, and self-modify their thinking and actions. Focusing can be associated with the constructivist theory of learning.

Examples:

What ideas can you come up with to build your structure?

How will you fill the area inside your structure?

What solutions can you think of to keep the blocks from falling?

What differences and similarities are there between your structure and the photo of the castle?

Powerful learning experiences can occur when you understand your questioning approaches, are able to organize and implement constructive questioning series, and can scaffold a student's thinking within a specific time and context. Engagement in high-level questioning patterns and interactions can lead to children developing the capacity to think and make decisions on their own (cognitive autonomy) and the ability to self-evaluate and self-modify their thinking and behaviors (cognitive flexibility). Cognitive autonomy and cognitive flexibility are two internal mechanisms needed to be successful in any educational setting. As teachers continually reflect on the questioning patterns they implement in the classroom with the students, they can begin to analyze, evaluate, and modify their questioning approach practices, thereby transforming and enhancing their inquiry capabilities, methodologies, and confidence.

The following are two partial questioning approach charts and graphs (fig. 5.10) that demonstrate the differences in how two teachers can engage children. Analyze and interpret the interactions based on the data.

Two Partial Questioning Approach Charts and Graphs

Teacher #1 Questioning Approach (Initiate – Respond – Feedback (IRF), Funneling, Focusing)	Teacher #2 Questioning Approach (Initiate – Respond – Feedback (IRF), Funneling, Focusing)
IRF	IRF
Funneling	IRF
Funneling	IRF
Focusing	IRF
Focusing	IRF
IRF	IRF
Focusing	IRF
Funneling	IRF
Funneling	IRF
Focusing	IRF
IRF	IRF
Funneling	IRF
Funneling	Funneling
Focusing	IRF
Funneling	IRF
"	"

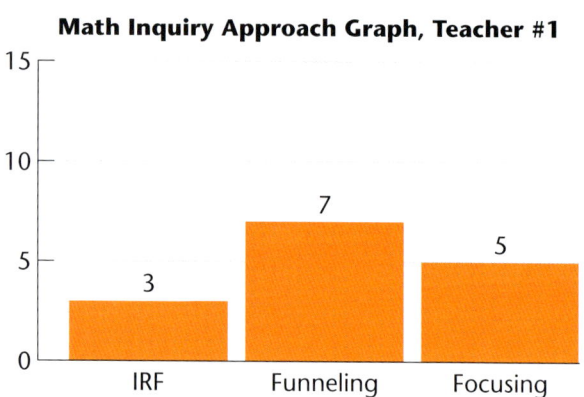

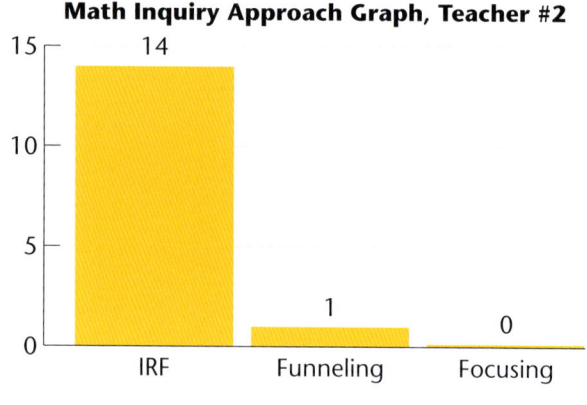

Figure 5.10b.

Figure 5.10a.

Based on this data, teacher #1 provided more child-centered, cognitively demanding questions to the group of children she was engaging. Even though the questions themselves are not provided, by understanding the kinds of questioning approaches that exist and knowing the implications they have on children's cognitive development, teachers gain an important perspective and a great starting point for reflecting upon the quality of the inquiry.

Questioning Content

The questioning content provided during teacher/child interactions is the second component teachers can examine. Teachers consider each question they have asked children during an interval of time and determine whether or not it was of mathematical significance and value. The importance of this procedure is enormous as the proficient teacher can target specific math topics and immerse the students in a continual flow of questions that support, sustain, and construct the mathematical ideas, theories, and concepts the children have decided to investigate.

When reflecting upon these questioning content charts and graphs (fig. 5.11), several patterns and perspectives emerge. First, it is clear when comparing both tables that the number and frequency of math questions is much greater in the teacher #1 chart. The majority of questions in the teacher #2 table are labeled "other," meaning that they were nonmathematical and may have been for social or an additional content area focus, such as science or social studies. Second, and just as important, are the sets of concept-based patterns that are seen in both the tables and graphs. The teacher #1 table and graph portray a questioning interaction by a teacher who explicitly focused and targeted the mathematical concepts the children investigated over a long period of time. By providing focused, ongoing, and sustained

Two Partial Questioning Content Charts and Graphs

Teacher #1 Questioning Contents (Numbers, Operations, Geometry, Algebra, Measurement)	Teacher #2 Questioning Contents (Numbers, Operations, Geometry, Algebra, Measurement)
Length Concept	Spatial Concept
Length Concept	Other (non-math)
Length Concept	Other (non-math)
Length Concept	Other (non-math)
Length Concept	Other (non-math)
Length Concept	Number Concept
Spatial Concept	Other (non-math)
Height Concept	Other (non-math)
Height Concept	Other (non-math)
Height Concept	Number Concept
Height Concept	Spatial Concept
Spatial Concept	Spatial Concept
Other (non-math)	Other (non-math)
Time Concept	Other (non-math)
Spatial Concept	Other (non-math)
"	"

Figure 5.11a.

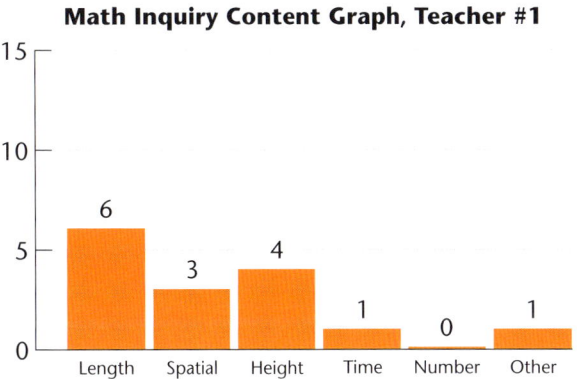

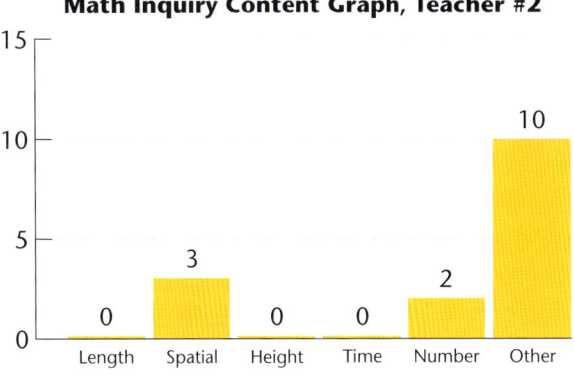

Figure 5.11b.

questioning content patterns, a teacher can ensure the students are acquiring knowledge and making sense of key math concepts. Lastly, beyond the previous two performance factors, teacher #1 also implemented and developed multiple math concept patterns. The concepts of length and height were being investigated and extended for a long period of time, meaning that there could be a high probability that children would begin to develop intimate relationships with two concepts that they are sure to encounter throughout their academic career.

Questioning Type

Closed-ended and open-ended questions are considered types of questions. They function as question formats. This means that the way a question is presented is intentionally limiting or limitless for the students. Closed-ended questions can be used during interactions to elicit specific information, seek facts, and help students think deeply about a problem at hand. They can also work as a catalyst for framing and initiating conversations; redirecting students' attention to specific topics, ideas, and processes; and helping summarize children's theories, conjectures, and findings. Open-ended questions, on the other hand, can be incorporated during conversations to promote deeper thought and obtain more elaborate responses from the students. They serve the critical role of creative thinking and have the most potential for cognitive growth and autonomy. Both types of questions serve important purposes and can be incorporated strategically and intentionally during daily lessons, routines, and projects to encourage opinions, promote discourse competence, and develop higher-level thinking.

The questioning type chart and graphs (fig. 5.12) pinpoint the number of times both open- and closed-ended questions were used by teachers during two separate ten-minute interactions with children where math was the focus. Based on the questioning type patterns, open-ended questions constituted the majority of teacher #1's questions. This signifies that the teacher placed the greater part of the thinking in the children's court. By asking open-ended questions, the teacher ensured that the cognitive processing required to reason and problem solve occurred in the minds of the children, thereby promoting students' abilities to think and develop cognitive autonomy.

The majority of teacher #2's questions, on the other hand, were mostly closed-ended, which may contain multiple meanings. First, it could mean that the children were incapable of responding to the teacher's questions during the interaction; therefore, the adult either modeled or coached the children through the thinking process. Second, it could indicate a lack of questioning and inquiry skills on the side of the adult. To be able to generate, implement, and sustain in-depth questioning patterns within any context is a very demanding task, and it takes proficient and expert teachers years to master the art of inquiry. Whichever the case may be, being able to pinpoint one's own questioning type patterns can provide insight into a teacher's current questioning strengths and needs.

> The questioning patterns chart helped me become much more cognizant and intentional about whether I am doing the thinking or asking my students to do the thinking. As I have grown in my ability to ask precise questions, my students' willingness to participate and add their thoughts and ideas to conversations with me and their peers has also developed. It's truly helped create a community of thinkers. —**Master Teacher Tamara Van Schoyck**

Two Partial Questioning Type Charts and Graphs

Teacher #1 Questioning Type (Closed-Ended vs. Open-Ended)	Teacher #2 Questioning Type (Closed-Ended vs. Open-Ended)
Closed	Closed
Closed	Closed
Open	Closed
Open	Open
Open	Closed
Open	Closed
Open	Closed
Closed	Closed
Open	Closed
Open	Closed
Open	Closed
Open	Closed
Open	Closed
Closed	Closed
Open	Closed
"	"

Figure 5.12a.

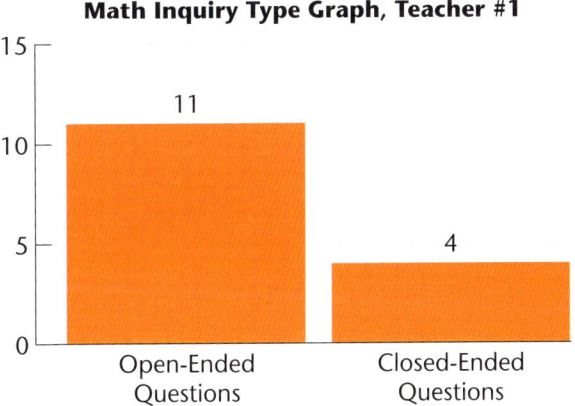

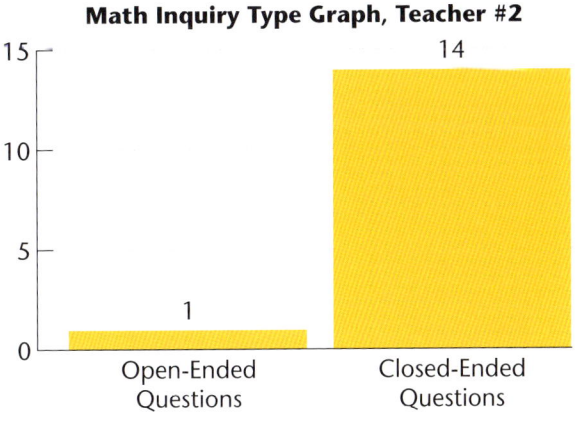

Figure 5.12b.

Questioning Styles

Teachers' questions with the main purpose of leading children to self-inquiry and self-directed problem solving are considered productive questions and are categorized on the Questioning Patterns chart as "questioning style" questions. *Style* in this context signifies the style of thinking the teacher wants children to engage in. As teachers guide students through the process of understanding a concept or creation, a harmonious tune of questioning patterns must be incorporated, where the teacher weaves in and out of the children's thought processes, asking the perfect style of questions to help them make meaning and construct knowledge on their own.

Here are the seven questioning styles that can work well when focusing on mathematical concepts:

- attention-focusing
- quantifying
- spatial relations
- comparison
- problem-posing
- reasoning
- proof

The style of questions chart (fig. 5.14), adapted from Mary Lee Martens's productive science questions chart (Martens 1999, 26), was created to define and illustrate the purpose of each style of question within a mathematical context. The style of questioning chart is arranged systematically in which the thinking involved in each dimension becomes more cognitively demanding as the list of styles progresses. This means that attention-focusing, quantifying, and spatial relations questions, though very important, are considered undemanding thinking processes compared to comparison, problem-posing, reasoning, and proof questions, which promote critical thinking and require more elaborate, precise, and accurate responses.

Styles of Math Questions

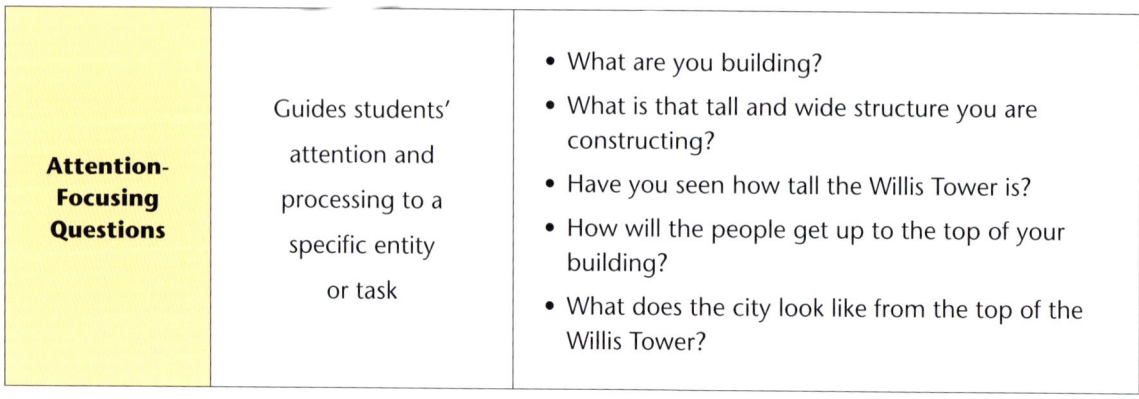

Attention-Focusing Questions	Guides students' attention and processing to a specific entity or task	• What are you building? • What is that tall and wide structure you are constructing? • Have you seen how tall the Willis Tower is? • How will the people get up to the top of your building? • What does the city look like from the top of the Willis Tower?

Figure 5.13.

Quantifying Questions	Guides students' attention and processing to a magnitude or multitude	• How many blocks are you going to add? • How tall are you going to build your tower? • How wide does the door have to be for the cars to be able to pass through? • How much time does it take to reach the top of the tower? • How many people fit inside the skyscraper?
Spatial Relations Questions	Encourages students to manipulate mental shapes and forms in space	• Which blocks can be used to construct a castle? • Which of the shapes are identical to each other? • What direction is the car driving? • Where would your final destination be if you followed that path? • Which set of cubes is part of the pattern?
Comparison Questions	Guides students' attention to analyzing multitudes or magnitudes	• What is the difference between the two castles? • How are the castles the same? • Can you compare the height of the castles with a ruler? • Can the two castles be joined together? • Which castle holds more people in it?
Problem-Posing Questions	Challenges students' abilities to plan and solve problems	• How will you be able to construct a castle with blocks and paper? • Is there a way to fill the foundation of the castle? • Can you find another solution to the falling blocks problem? • Can you figure out how to connect the four walls together? • Can you try another way to build the perimeter of the castle?

Figure 5.13. cont'd

Reasoning Questions	Promotes students' justification or explanation skills	• Why are you placing some blocks vertically and some horizontally? • Can you tell me why your castle is missing doors and windows? • What is your reason for building three levels? • Why do you think the third level keeps collapsing? • Why did you choose to connect the two castles?
Proof Questions	Promotes students' factual justification, validation, and explanation skills	• How many inches long is the castle? • How many units taller is the first castle than the second castle? • How many more dominoes where used in this train track? • How many more students preferred the block castle than the clay castle? • How can you prove your conjecture is correct?

Figure 5.13. cont'd

The following are two questioning style graphs (fig. 5.14) that were created for teachers to reflect on their performance. Examine and deduce the quality of the styles of thinking the two teachers promoted in the classroom while interacting with individuals and small groups of students.

The two questioning style graphs can demonstrate some major educational viewpoints. When we compare the two teachers' questioning style patterns, teacher #1 seemed to focus more on the cognitively demanding questions. This has significant repercussions for the students involved in the interaction. If we were to extrapolate the data from these sets of learning and thinking patterns, we would conclude that the students engaged with teacher #1 are being prepared to think at a higher cognitive level, due to the number and frequency of demanding questions being incorporated. Students engaged with teacher #2 are being lead to think about a specific action or concept, as the teacher provided mostly attention-focusing questions; therefore, at this stage, the children are involved but with mostly undemanding thinking processes.

Two Teacher Questioning Style Charts and Graphs

Teacher #1 Questioning Style (Attention-Focusing, Quantifying, Spatial Relations, Comparison, Problem-Posing, Reasoning, Proof)	Teacher #2 Questioning Style (Attention-Focusing, Quantifying, Spatial Relations, Comparison, Problem-Posing, Reasoning, Proof)
Attention-Focusing	Attention-Focusing
Problem-Posing	Attention-Focusing
Problem-Posing	Attention-Focusing
Reasoning	Reasoning
Reasoning	Attention-Focusing
Attention-Focusing	Attention-Focusing
Quantifying	Attention-Focusing
Attention-Focusing	Attention-Focusing
Problem-Posing	Attention-Focusing
Problem-Posing	Attention-Focusing
Problem-Posing	Attention-Focusing
Reasoning	Attention-Focusing
Problem-Posing	Attention-Focusing
Reasoning	Attention-Focusing
Attention-Focusing	Attention-Focusing
"	"

Figure 5.14a.

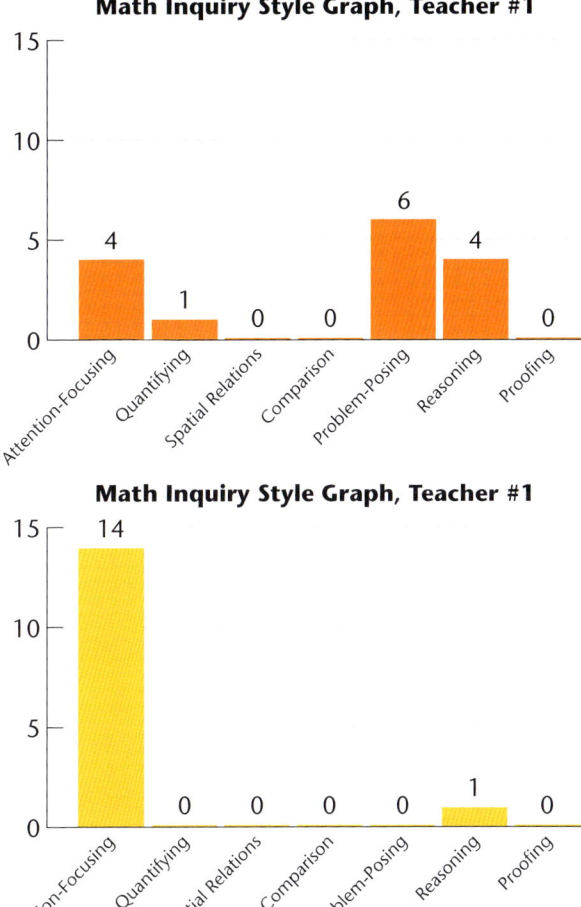

Figure 5.15b.

Based on charting, analyzing, and evaluating the rest of the styles of questions the teachers provided during the ten-minute exercise, a principal or education director could conclude the kind of professional development each teacher would need, as well as be able to assist the teachers in planning for future inquiry-based engagements with the students. When teachers can instantaneously generate intentional questions and apply them within children's daily lives, the classroom-thinking culture can change into a dynamic atmosphere where students value the perspectives of their peers and learn to collaborate in more constructive and productive interactions.

INQUIRY-BASED INTERACTION

The following interaction occurred while I was working with a six-year-old kindergarten child interested in knights, kings, and castles. You will notice how I incorporated the various questioning components—approach, content, type, and styles (ACTS)—to help him think and problem solve throughout the construction challenge.

Child: *I'm going to make a castle with the blocks.*

Allen: *What design pattern ideas do you have for constructing your structure?*

Child: *Well, I would like to build a tall castle for the king and his knights.*

Allen: *Would you like me to provide you with a challenge?*

Child: *Yes, I love challenges!*

Allen: *Okay! How about constructing a castle that is three levels high?*

Child: *Three levels high? That is a challenge. . . . Okay, let's get to work! I'm going to use the long blocks to build the walls and the ceiling. One, two, three, . . . eleven, twelve! And now the top. One, two, three, four. There, I created the first level. Now I have to build the second level. One, two, three, . . . seven, eight. And now the top. . . . Oh no, I ran out of long blocks and now I can't add the ceiling.*

Figure 5.15. Kindergartners' completed 3-level castle with "the guardian knights and the king's chamber on the top level"

Allen: *Why can't you add the ceiling?*

Child: *Because the walls are too far apart and I ran out of long blocks. The medium blocks don't fit. Look . . . see they are not long enough and they fall down. Maybe if I put the medium blocks together it will fit? No, it doesn't fit. What am I going to do now? I don't have any more long blocks for the ceiling.*

Allen: *How are your long blocks being used right now?*

Child: *I used them for the first level. Look, the long blocks make the wall and the ceiling, but I don't have enough for the second-level ceiling.*

Allen: *So, you are telling me that you used all the long blocks for the first-level walls and ceiling, and that you need the long blocks to complete the second-level* ceiling. Can you think of any ideas that would allow you to use the long blocks on your second-level ceiling?

Child: *No, all the long blocks are being used for the first level.*

Allen: *Well, do you see any size patterns with the short, medium, and long blocks?*

Child: *They are just different sizes.*

Allen: *What happens if you stand them next to each other? Do you see any size patterns that can give you some ideas?*

Child: *Wait! I see a pattern! If you add two medium-size blocks together they make the same size as the long block. I can switch the long blocks with the two medium-size blocks.*

Allen: *Great thinking! Way to solve the problem!*

Child: *Yes! That's why I love challenges because I get to use my thinking skills.*

Allen: *That's right! You're using your thinking skills to solve problems. So what is your next idea for building your castle?*

Child: *Well, I'm going to have to switch all these blocks in the back with the medium-size blocks and use the long blocks to make the ceiling.*

Allen: *Good thinking. Let's see how your idea turns out. (Child switches the blocks from the first level and adds them to the second level.)*

Child: *There! I finished the second level and now I can make the third level.*

Allen: *Do you think the foundation is strong enough to hold the third level?*

Child: *I think so. . . . As long as you are very careful putting the blocks on top, they shouldn't fall. (The structure starts rocking side to side, and some of the blocks fall down as the child adds the blocks on the third level.)*

Allen: *What happened? Why did some of the blocks fall down?*

Child: *I don't know. I'm trying to put the blocks softly, but they keep falling down. I don't know what else to do.*

Allen: *Well, let's look at the foundation. Do you think the blocks of the castle are aligned?*

Child: *I think so.*

Allen: *How can you tell if the blocks are aligned?*

Child: *Or maybe not because the pieces are falling.*

Allen: *Let's look at the first level. What do you notice about the blocks sustaining the castle?*

Child: *Let's see. Hmm . . . I see, the ones in the middle are loose. They are not the same as the front.*

Allen: *How can you make the middle blocks the same as the front blocks?*

Child: *I think I need to line them up together so they are the same.*

Allen: *Okay, let's test your idea.*

Child: *There, now they are lined up.*

Allen: *How about the second level? Do you see any unaligned blocks?*

Child: *Let's see . . . Yup! The middle blocks are loose and crooked. . . . There, now my castle is aligned. (The child continues and completes the third level.) I'm done! Now I can add a king at each level, and the knights will protect the kings from the bad guys.*

During this interaction, I strategically challenged the child to build a three-level structure, knowing that he would either run out of the long- or medium-size blocks. By analyzing the properties and attributes of the materials prior to a child interacting with them, a teacher can generate probable problem-solving scenarios that may arise when the student becomes engaged with them. This strategy can be useful when a teacher wants to plan for the type of creative and critical thinking they want their students to engage in and develop. The "challenge" approach implemented in this interaction also promoted cognitive conflict (the process of making sense of new ideas or facts) and cognitive flexibility (the ability to self-evaluate and self-modify your own thinking and behaviors), which are also critical elements of constructivism (Piaget 1985; Bruner 1986). The process of providing new information that conflicts with a child's background knowledge can lead to a child becoming motivated to the point of finding *equilibrium,* or the truth. In this case, I was prepared to expect the following problems as the child constructed a multilayered structure with the blocks.

Probable Problem-Solving Scenarios Chart

- Child runs out of long-size blocks and will have to figure out how to use two medium blocks (part-to-whole concept) to obtain the same length results needed for further construction.
- Child runs out of medium-size blocks and will have to figure out the part-to-whole concept with the small-size blocks.
- Child runs into a challenge while aligning/balancing three levels of wall and ceiling blocks and will have to figure out the arrangement of the blocks in relative position to each other and find the center of gravity of the connecting blocks.
- Child will have to use perception and background knowledge to create the mental picture of the structure he decides to represent with blocks.
- Child will have to make the logical connections between the characters and the setting he is role-playing and creating.
- Child may become frustrated, so the educator intervenes by allowing the child to express his anxieties and by targeting the problem with guiding/constructive questions to help facilitate the child's problem-solving process.
- Child may need positive reinforcement throughout the construction to help him keep focused on the task.

Figure 5.16.

By generating these seven probable problem-solving scenarios, I was able to

- identify the probable problems that may arise;
- generate solutions to the problems;
- research sophisticated language to be incorporated during the process;
- generate open-ended questions to be asked as problems arise; and
- develop constructive questions for the child to think about as he reflects on his steps and actions during the process of construction.

The process of generating and creating probable problem-solving scenarios and solutions is a great strategy for teachers to become active thinkers and participants in the play before, during, and after the child's construction process. It mentally and intellectually prepares the teacher to engage the child at a higher cognitive level.

Emphasizing Proof Skills

Proof is the process of validating a fact or truth about an idea, topic, or concept through evidence or an argument. Proof skills could be emphasized more often at the early childhood level, as they help in developing children's deeper understanding of mathematics. The skill of providing simple proofs allows children to look at ideas, concepts, and creations with more detail. The process of explaining and establishing the validity of a hypothesis encourages children to continue delving into an investigation. This, in turn, helps students refine their thinking and actions.

The principles and standards from the National Council of Teachers of Mathematics (NCTM 2000) suggests that we "use various types of reasoning and methods of proof." At the early childhood level, different types of reasoning and proof methods can include the following:

- discourse
- pictures
- graphs
- any other form of communication that can explicitly justify children's thinking

In the following interaction, our kindergarten friend from the previous knights, kings, and castle construction (fig. 5.15), is now a beginning first grader, and uses reasoning and proof skills to think about and develop his drawing of the Teatro Municipale, a theatre in Reggio Emilia, Italy.

REGGIO EMILIA OPERA HOUSE DRAWINGS (BEGINNING FIRST GRADER)

Figure 5.17. Reggio Emilia Opera House, Reggio Emilia, Italy

Allen: *What do you think about this photo?*

Child: *Well, it's very beautiful. I like the way the lights are different colors and sizes. The lights look like living spirits, and the things on top of the building look like people. Is that you on the top of the building on the far end? It looks like you. I really like the sky's color, and the tree looks dark and gloomy. I think I'd like to draw a picture of this place. It looks really cool.*

Allen: *Tell me about your drawing.*

Child: *First I drew the building, and I added the windows, doors, columns, and some lights. Then I added the lights on the bottom, and I kept the same pattern as I saw on the photo. I drew the trees and the sky, and finally I shaded in the dark space on the bottom by the lights and on the building.*

Allen: *Let's compare your drawing to the photo. Do you see anything different, and would you add or change something to your drawing?*

Child: *Well, the building is bigger on the photo, and I missed some columns. One, two, three, . . . ten. Also, the shade of the building, the trees, and the fountain are different on the photo, and on my picture they look the same.*

Allen: *How can we make the size of your building and the shading of your objects more precise?*

Child: *Let me measure the size of the building with a ruler. The building is eight inches wide and four inches tall on the photo, so I will have to make the building bigger. I think I will draw the picture again and shade the areas with different colors, and I will add more pressure to the pencil so that the color is much stronger.*

Figure 5.18. First drawing of Reggio Emilia Opera House

Figure 5.19. Second drawing of Reggio Emilia Opera House

In this interaction, the child's reasoning and proof skills allowed him to think creatively and critically about his creation. His skills also helped him develop the composition with more detail. By recognizing and assessing the differences in proportion, perspectives, and the various elements in the photograph, he was able to reason why his drawing looked different. In order to justify, explain, and provide proof of the difference, he used a ruler to prove his opinion. Once he justified his opinion, he used the new proven facts to refine and create a new more precise drawing.

You can increase children's ability to develop and apply reasoning and proof skills by seeing the learning possibilities in every interaction. Opportunities can arise within mathematical contexts such as children creating and constructing with materials, the various forms of play, small- and large-group reflection sessions, and many other contexts. By employing a broad range of intentional and precise questioning, you can guide children to deeper levels of understanding and insight. Through experiences similar to this drawing interaction, students can learn to explain and justify their actions, allowing them to develop positive dispositions toward thinking and learning.

Some further examples of promoting reasoning and proof skills occurred in the following situations. As children took part in a planting seeds project, they predicted the size of the plant growth and validated their statements by charting their observations on a daily growth chart. In another classroom, children created a rainbow pattern with Lego Duplo bricks, which are double the size of standard Lego bricks. The teacher asked children to estimate how many standard-size Legos it would take to create the same-size rainbow pattern made with the larger Legos. The children estimated and provided their reasoning for why they thought their amount was correct. They then proceeded to validate their estimations by creating the new rainbow pattern and counting the total number of standard-size Legos it took to recreate the structure. A final example where a teacher promoted children's reasoning and proof skills occurred during a food experience. The teacher brought her juicer machine from home and two dozen oranges for the children to experience fresh juice. She placed many eight-ounce cups on the table and asked children to estimate how many cups of juice twenty-four oranges would produce. The children estimated, explained their reasoning, and validated their results after the juicer squeezed and the juice filled five cups.

The examples provided throughout the book showcase the different ways that teachers have incorporated reasoning and proof skills within their interactions with preschool children, from Mrs. Molina's rainbow project (page 4), where the children predicted the length of the rainbow and validated the results by measuring the length of the lines, to Mrs. Carrasquillo's machine study (page 24), where children estimated and measured the distance that the objects traveled. The possibility of promoting these thinking skills are endless in early childhood settings. You just have to make it a habit to ask children the reasoning behind their thinking and actions, as well as promote the importance of proving their facts through the process of using evidence to justify their stance.

CREATING PROTOCOLS FOR GROUP METACOGNITION AND REFLECTIVE PRACTICE

Group metacognition is the process of students working together to solve complex problems before, during, and after an activity by planning, monitoring, and evaluating the learning processes through group collaboration (Goos et al. 2002; Hinsz 2004; Chalmers 2009). Research indicates that group learning and collaboration can promote higher-level thinking as students share ideas, strategies, and understandings, and learn to solve complex mathematical problems through communication and group skills (Curtis and Carter 2007; Johnson and Johnson 2012; Gillies 2007). Reflective practice in the early childhood classroom is the process of children (and teachers) reflecting critically on their experiences, ideas, and concepts. It is an opportunity to improve knowledge and understandings (Ayas and Zeniuk 2001); evaluate one's "beliefs, assumptions, and hypotheses" (Dewey 1933, 6–7); reflect in action, during the experience, and reflect on action, after the experience (Schön 1983); and learn to share and accept each other's different perspectives (Moran 1998).

The following Group Metacognition and Reflective Process diagram (fig. 5.20) illustrates several key factors and ideas. First, it establishes the relationship between metacognition (thinking about thinking) and reflection (thinking about actions) as communal and fundamental components of a learning study's process. Metacognition is the process that occurs when teachers and children implement strategies to monitor learning. This means that learners intentionally stop before, during, or after an activity to evaluate whether they understood the content.

Reflection adds another element, as it can be described as the learning process that occurs when group members reflect critically on their actions and the topics connected to their ideas, values, and beliefs. When both elements are used simultaneously throughout a study's steps and phases, teachers allow children to be absorbed in thought and collaboration, which can develop the passion for learning. Second, the diagram illustrates critical teaching and learning components that teachers can incorporate harmoniously for great learning experiences to transpire. When teachers integrate pedagogical elements such as the ones found in learning/thinking protocols, project/problem-based learning, and collaborative-inquiry processes, children's capacities to learn flourish. Lastly and equally important, is the fact that group metacognition and reflection is a process, and teachers need to understand the elements in both processing styles to be able to facilitate children's mathematical learning at each phase of a learning study.

Group Metacognition and Reflective Process diagram

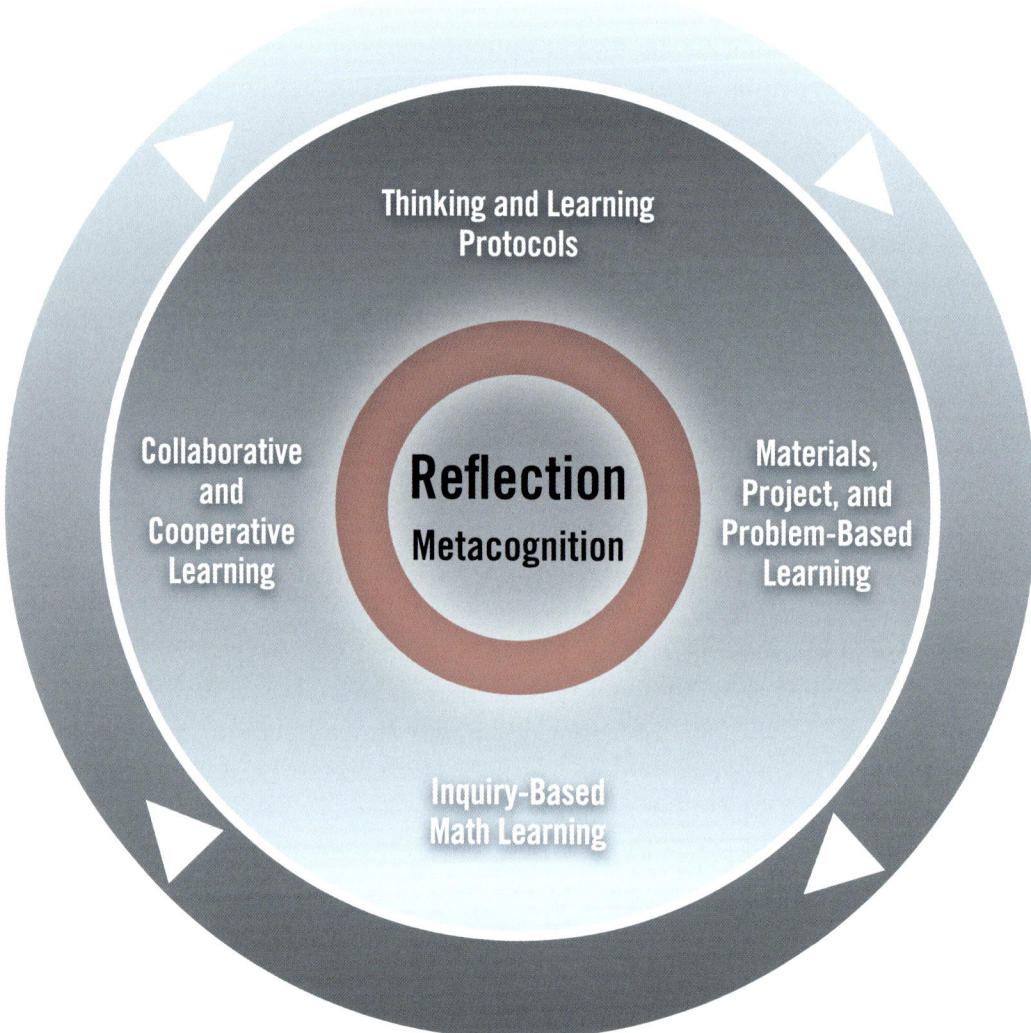

Figure 5.20.

The roles of the teachers and children involved in group metacognition and reflection can differ according to age and class level. Nevertheless, the thinking and collaborative learning processing and goals remain the same across all levels. For optimal learning to occur with early childhood students, teachers can incorporate the following four components during play or project work:

- creating thinking and learning protocols to help monitor students' thinking (group metacognition), and establishing a culture of reflective practice in the classroom (Bodrova and Leong 2007; Weiser 2008; Hiebert et al. 1997);

- providing open-ended and complex projects, problems, and materials that promote high levels of collaboration (Edwards, Gandini and Forman 1998; Zawojewski, Lesh, and English 2003; Helm and Katz 2010);

- engaging children through an inquiry-based learning approach (Dewey 1938; Bruner 1961; Piaget 1984);

- developing children's collaborative and cooperative learning skills to be able to work as a social unit and develop holonomous classroom communities (Copley 2001; Featherstone et al. 2011; Forman and Fyfe 2012).

THINKING AND LEARNING PROTOCOLS

The creation and implementation of thinking and learning protocols by teachers is a powerful method that supports the development of children's intellectual abilities and academic skills. This involves a teacher creating a multistep sequence of learning experiences (pages 99–101, 104–106, 107–109) that scaffold students' actions and thinking processes based on their interests and ideas. This style of methodology aligns with the cognitivism proposed by Jean Piaget (1936, 1964); Jerome Bruner (1986); and Lev Vygotsky (1962), where teachers scaffold and develop children's mental processes sequentially, strategically, and intentionally. By organizing the actions and thinking a group of students will engage in, teachers can ensure that individuals will be provided with the opportunity to develop basic and advanced thinking skills that can help them become confident and proficient learners.

> Protocols provide my ELL students the opportunity to express their understanding of a concept using a variety of art media. In doing so I'm able to successfully gauge ELL students' background knowledge and facilitate scaffolding to deepen their understanding of that concept. —**Master Teacher Tyler Flynn-Rambo**

Thinking protocols (page 99) are sequenced-based, guided forms of activities that explicitly develop children's thinking skills and content-area base knowledge. Teachers can design various types of thinking protocols by using

Bloom's Taxonomy of Learning Objectives (fig. 5.21) (Anderson et al. 2000) to plan for the type of thinking children will experience. Adults can also use the six categories to ask intentional questions aimed at facilitating children's explorations and investigations. Thinking protocols are important because they help teach, organize, and scaffold students' mental processes. In the case of mathematics they also build the academic structures needed for future academic success.

Bloom's Taxonomy of Learning Objectives is one of the most influential curriculum tools in the education field. The following adaptation was created to demonstrate the thinking processes according to their degree of difficulty and to align the cognitive processing to a mathematical perspective.

Bloom's Taxonomy of Learning Objectives

Figure 5.21. Bloom's Taxonomy Math Wheel illustration

The following thinking protocol was created to help students in the process of learning about the structure of theatres, which had been a highly talked about topic among the children. Mrs. Rosales's preschool classroom engaged in this two-week thinking protocol that was provided as part of their theatre study.

Thinking Protocol (Theatre Study)

1. Construct: Allow children (small group) to construct a theatre with blocks through their own imagination and to role-play their chosen characters (fig. 5.22).

2. Identify: Observe a photo of a theatre (whole group) and identify the elements they see in the photograph. The teacher writes a list of the children's responses on chart paper (fig. 5.23).

3. Draw: Draw the theatre (individually) and add as many elements as the children remember identifying in the photograph. The teacher writes down and labels children's responses (fig. 5.24).

Figure 5.22. Children's first theatre construction

Figure 5.23. Children identify elements in a theatre photo.

Figure 5.24. Children draw the elements identified in the theatre photo.

4. Describe: Observe a photo of the theatre (whole group) and describe the mathematical properties and attributes they see in the photograph. The teacher writes a list of the children's responses on chart paper (fig. 5.25).

5. Construct: Allow children (small group) to construct a theatre with blocks on their own and to role-play their chosen characters (fig. 5.26).

6. Analyze: Add a photo layer of children's previously constructed structure to original photo and have children (whole group) analyze the composition (fig. 5.27).

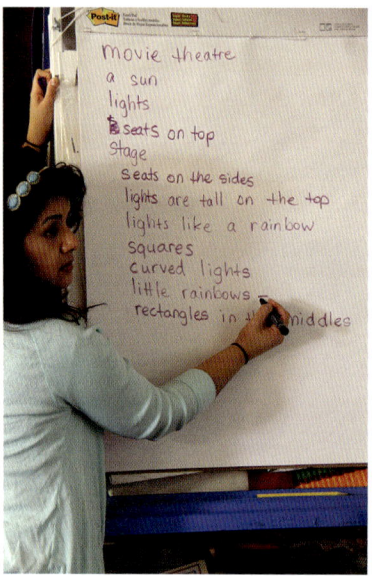

Figure 5.25. Children describe the mathematical properties and attributes found in the photo.

Figure 5.26. Children construct the elements they described.

Figure 5.27. Children analyze a new composition of the theatre photograph that depicts the center seating section constructed in blocks.

7. Compare: Children (whole group) compare the properties and attributes of two different theatres. The teacher creates a Venn diagram to illustrate simple set relationships between the two theatres (fig. 5.28).

8. Construct: Allow children (small group) to construct a theatre with blocks. The teacher provides constructive questions based on what the group described on the photo of the theatre (fig. 5.29).

9. Assess: The students (small group) diagnose what part of the construction is working well and what challenges they are confronting. The teacher writes a list of the children's responses on chart paper (fig. 5.30).

10. Explain: Children present and explain (whole group) what they learned, how they were able to construct their theatres, and why they were able to be successful (fig. 5.31).

Figure 5.28. Children compare and discuss the mathematical differences and similarities between the original theatre photo and a new theatre photo; a Venn diagram is created.

Figure 5.29. Children construct a model based on the new theatre photo.

Figure 5.30. Children assess what works well and what doesn't.

Figure 5.31. Children share their learning experiences from the theatre study with their classmates.

Thinking Protocol (Theatre Study)

This two-week thinking protocol presented and implemented in the classroom with students is one effective way of processing and learning higher-level mathematics, as it challenges and requires students to learn about the patterns, relationships, and mathematical functions in the network of concepts found in structure. Children were guided and provided with the necessary learning experiences needed to understand and make sense of the mathematical elements found in architecture, allowing them to

- *identify* the objects in the photo (quantify);
- *describe* the mathematical properties and attributes of the identified elements (magnitude, multitude);
- *construct* structures throughout the study (number sense, measurement, algebra); and
- *analyze* processes, learning, and the constructed structures.

Thinking protocols are dynamic in that teachers can develop multiple kinds of protocols based on the type of mathematical content teachers and students want to learn. There are specific math concepts and processing that will occur during constructive play such as the theatre protocol presented above. Another type of protocol can be developed as a way of targeting the mathematical learning that will take place in dramatic play. For example, children that represent cooking scenarios can benefit from a protocol that focuses on the

- distance traveled between the home and grocery store;
- quantifying of the amount of groceries needed;
- measurement (size, weight) of the grocery items chosen;
- price and purchasing procedures of the items;
- estimating (amount) and measuring (temperature) of the food items to be cooked; and
- serving (number operations) of the deliciously prepared cuisine children may create.

Through these interactions and experiences, the children can develop an understanding of the mathematical patterns, relationships, and functions in the network of concepts found in the culinary arts. The possibility of creating focused-thinking protocols are endless and the study topics extensive.

Learning protocols are similar to thinking protocols in that they both are planned sequential-learning experiences that engage children in multidimensional learning processes and are based on the students' interests. However, learning protocols are more open-ended in terms of the children's journey, as the various kinds of materials provided and the children's interests drive the process. The children are in complete control of their learning studies, and the teacher understands that the optimal goal of this process is the learning that arises from the creative process.

For some teachers it may be difficult to let go of the control found in teacher-directed instruction; however, when one analyzes and reflects upon the powerful mental activity that children process while creating with materials, it becomes clear that children's intellectual propensity, dexterity, and aptitude are being developed. Likewise, embedded in the creative process, one finds an abundance of mathematical perspectives and thinking processes that must be discovered, investigated, and understood. These cognitively demanding processes work best when teachers allow children to create and construct their interests with materials in contexts they have chosen.

The mathematical elements found in structure and function within our environments can work as catalysts for children's studies. When students create and have multiple opportunities to represent their learning through materials, their understanding of the world around them deepens. Learning protocols can strategically support children's studies by providing the opportunities to make sense of their environment through respectful and purposeful processes. The following two learning protocols demonstrate part of the learning that transpired through children's creative mathematical studies.

LEARNING PROTOCOL (KINGDOM STUDY) (STRUCTURE AND FUNCTION)

1. Magnatiles and Legos: Invite students to create a structure based on their environment and interests (fig. 5.32).

2. Basswood: Encourage the children to construct and represent their interests from the first creation (fig. 5.33).

3. Balsa wood: Ask the students to create the next story or system relationship to extend the story (fig. 5.34).

Figure 5.32. The king's castle and twenty knights that protect the people

Figure 5.33. The bridge to the castle; the king and nine knights stand guard

Figure 5.34. Horse and cart that carries food from the farm to the castle

4. Clay, paper, soil: Revisit the children's story and allow them to create a representation of any new interests found inside their story with mixed media (fig. 5.35).

5. Balsa wood and clay: The children create a representation of the interests, topics, and concepts they have taken as a focal point (fig. 5.36).

6. Foam board and model grass: The students construct a representation of any new interests they want to graft into their continuing story (fig. 5.37).

7. Artist markers: The students revisit any interesting ideas from the story and create a second representation of any characters, structures, or functions (fig. 5.38).

Figure 5.35. Farmers gather their harvest for the people; the line patterns are carrots and potatoes that are growing inside the ground.

Figure 5.36. A well where the farmers collect water

Figure 5.37. Every kingdom needs a water purification plant.

Figure 5.38. A diagram showing water traveling over a mountain, into a lake, being purified by three machines, and ending up in a sink. (Two fishermen are shown on the lake.)

8. Clay and dowels: The students use mixed media to create a representation of an element they find interesting in their story (fig. 5.39).

9. Color pencils: The students invite other peers to draw and create a shared perspective regarding a structure or function in the story (fig. 5.40).

10. Artist markers: The children reflect on one of the structures in their kingdom and draw its functionality (fig. 5.41).

11. Final composition: The students compile all the story creations and display a final composition of their kingdom study (fig. 5.42).

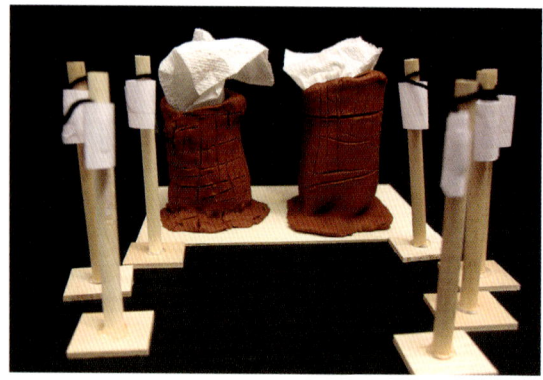

Figure 5.39. A nuclear power plant and transmission poles

Figure 5.40. A diagram showing the inside of the nuclear power plant

Figure 5.41. A transformer on a power pole that reduces the "size" of the electricity flow

Figure 5.42. A bird's-eye view of the entire, glorious kingdom

LEARNING PROTOCOL (KINGDOM STUDY) MATHEMATICAL PHYSICS IN URBAN ENGINEERING FOCUS

FINAL KINGDOM COMPOSITION

This is the kingdom. The king and the knights protect the kingdom from the bad guys. Everyone has to work to help each other. The farmers plant the food and go to the well to collect water in the buckets and water the vegetables. The drivers bring the vehicle to the farm, and the farmers put the carrots and potatoes inside the vehicle. The drivers take the food to the castle and have to ask the knights' permission to cross the bridge. The chef inside the castle cooks for everyone in the kingdom. He turns the stove on with electricity that comes from the power plant. He adds purified water that comes from the water purification plant to the pot. Then he adds the carrots and potatoes to the pot and cooks delicious soup. The king calls all the people inside the kingdom for dinner, and they are all friends.

MATHEMATICAL LITERATURE LEARNING PROTOCOL

1. Graphite pencil: Invite children to draw a story (one to three pages) based on their environment and interests (fig. 5.43).

2. Blocks: Encourage the children to construct and represent their interests from the stories they created (fig. 5.44).

Figure 5.43. "This is me and my family going to the Willis Tower. It is 108 stories tall!"

Figure 5.44. "This is what it looks like from the top of the Willis Tower. And that's my Luigi on a motorcycle."

3. Acrylic paint: Ask the students to create a painting representing their next topic of interest from their stories (fig. 5.45).

4. Recyclable materials: Revisit the children's stories and allow them to create representations of any new interests found inside their stories (fig. 5.46).

5. Wire: The children create representations of the interests/topics/concepts they have taken as focal points (fig. 5.47).

6. Wood/paint/recyclables: The students construct representations of any new interest they want to graft into their continuing stories (fig. 5.48).

Figure 5.45. "There are many doors in this city view. Inside the building there is a woman talking on the phone. There is a robot next to her."

Figure 5.46. "This robot is inside the building, and he's telling silly jokes. The woman does not appreciate the robot telling jokes."

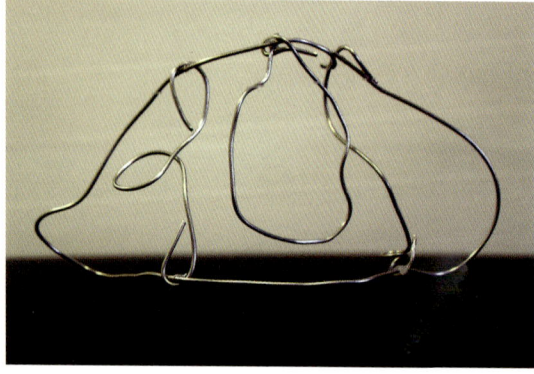

Figure 5.47. "This is the school and it has a door, stairs, and the principal is there. The lady called the principal because she's looking for a job. The robot is just too silly."

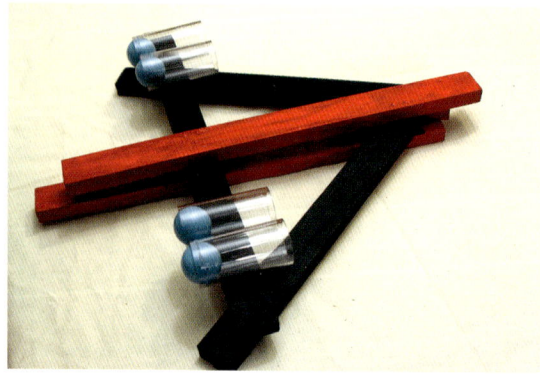

Figure 5.48. "This is the airplane, and the lady went on it so that she could get to her home fast."

7. Clay/wire: The students use mixed media to create representations of an element they find interesting in the story (fig. 5.49).

8. Metal: The students revisit any interesting ideas from the stories and create a second representation of any characters (fig. 5.50).

9. Artist marker/pastels: Each student invites a peer to draw and create a shared perspective they both find interesting in the story (fig. 5.51).

10. Photography: Each student completes the story by adding all the created works produced throughout the protocol into one final composition and narrating the story with a group of children (fig. 5.52).

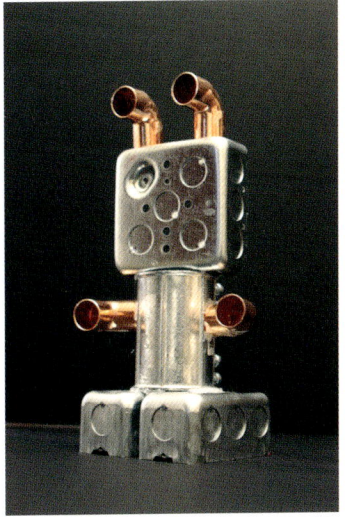

Figure 5.50. "The robot transformed and visited the lady at her home to apologize for irritating her with his behavior."

Figure 5.49. "This is the home. It is a castle with a tall tower that goes up to the sky."

Figure 5.51. "The lady and the robot are looking outside the castle. The trees and buildings look much bigger because they are on the first floor and not on the 103rd floor like at the Willis Tower."

Figure 5.52. "This is the last page of my story. They are all friends now, and they all went to the forest for a picnic. The family is very little because they are far away. They are close to the little trees next to them. The lady and the silver robot are holding hands and are playing hide-n-seek with the other robot. He is closing his eyes and counting to twenty. He won't be able to find them because they will be hiding inside the trees, but then they will surprise him. The mommy will then call the lady and the robots and invite them to dinner at the castle."

In both mathematical learning protocols, the children assumed complete control of the environments, stories, and creations. However, the teacher strategically planned the type of learning and extended the kind of thinking that would occur throughout the process. By intentionally providing the children with multiple types of materials and strategically increasing the complexity of the processing throughout the learning protocol, the teacher ensured the learning in the creative process was of great value. The adult also guided the children in the reflective process by revisiting and extending the students' creative stories, mathematical perspectives, and overall thinking.

Thinking and Learning Protocol Scope, Organization, and Purpose

Young children often become curious and interested in the structures and functions found in their immediate environment. They begin to represent their observations, ideas, and theories with the various learning media available in their classrooms. Children can spend an enormous amount of time creating structures with blocks, clay, drawing tools, and other creative media. They can also invest large amounts of time exploring the functions of structures through dramatization, which allows them to make sense of individuals' roles and purposes in life.

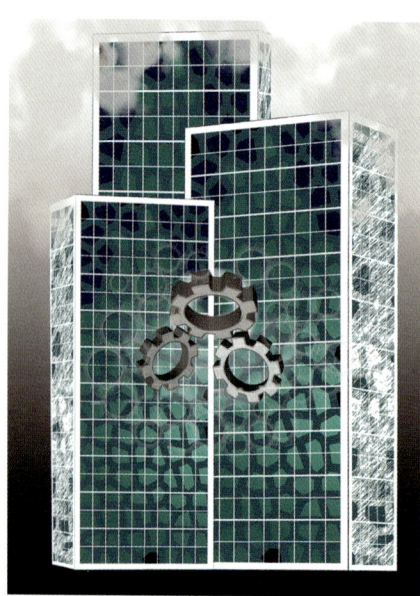

Figure 5.53. In this representation, structure (buildings) and function (gears) work together to generate and produce light (learning) for the system (society) it is intended to serve.

Teachers can use thinking and learning protocols to guide and develop students' understanding of the mathematical structures and functions found in any system. For example, a city can be considered a system with many structures such as buildings, transportation vehicles, power poles, traffic lights, and other physical structures. Though each type of structure within this system is constructed uniquely, they all share mathematical patterns and relationships. Skyscrapers in general share the same network of mathematical concepts such as height, width, depth, and their accompanying attributes. Likewise, each of the structures in a city has a positional or mechanical function. Skyscrapers have residential/commercial (apartments, stores, people) functions, as well as interior infrastructure (electrical, mechanical) functions. Transportation vehicles serve for both personal and professional purposes, power lines play vital roles in delivering electricity to homes, and traffic lights help motorists drive orderly and safely. Understanding the scope, organization, and purpose of protocols can support educators in seeing the "big picture" in children's potential learning opportunities that may arise within their environments.

Through the implementation of thinking and learning protocols, educators can ensure all children are provided with powerful learning experiences that promote students' abilities to

- engage in long-term studies;
- obtain knowledge and insight;
- develop meaningful relationships with colleagues; and
- acquire the love of learning.

Materials and Project- and Problem-Based Learning

Challenging projects and problems can emerge in the presence of working with creative and constructive materials. Pedagogically, providing great learning materials in the classroom and during lessons promotes different types of thinking and collaboration; therefore, teachers can plan to incorporate cognitively demanding materials in their lessons and engage children through group problem solving (Sarama and Clements 2009a), or by providing "provocatory" questioning (Rankin 1998, 218). Intentional work with materials also provides many opportunities for children to think mathematically as they explore the materials, develop conjectures as to the possibilities of working with the materials, and engage in representational work and development.

Project-based learning is an instructional approach that promotes children's active participation in the process of creating structures or systems found in real-life settings. This approach is student centered and develops children's problem-solving, collaboration, and reflection skills through small-group interactions. As projects with creative and constructive materials unfold, children are challenged to solve complex mathematical problems. At the same time, you can begin to guide students through the process of metacognition and reflection throughout the phases of the task.

Before children engage with materials, you can ask questions and provide activities to help students think about and plan how they will approach the project. You can ask questions such as

- How are you planning to construct the . . . ?
- What challenges do you see in the construction?
- How can you help each other during the construction?

- Can you represent how you will approach the construction? What similarities and differences do you see in each other's representations?

- What steps has the group chosen to begin the construction?

By providing children with provocatory and constructive questioning as an ongoing routine, children develop the ability to think of ideas and strategies before and during the engagement process of the project.

Problem-based learning shares many processing characteristics as project-based learning methodology with one major difference: a "problem" establishes the focus for the group of learners. For example, after the completion of a project where a small group of children construct a castle out of blocks, a teacher can challenge the group by posing probable problems:

- What can we build so that the princess can reach the tenth floor?

- What can we construct to help the farmers transport the harvest from the field to the castle as fast as possible?

- What can we create to help the kingdom produce electricity for all the people's homes?

As small groups of children are given the materials and the time to construct solutions, many ideas and processes begin to emerge and develop, leading to higher levels of thinking and collaborative learning.

Challenging children's learning with complex mathematical, creative, and critical-thinking systems such as the ones found in material exploration, and project- and problem-based learning methodologies can provide the real-life experiences that children will need in order to make sense of the abstract concepts they are required to learn in elementary school settings. As young children enter the lower elementary school grades, they will be required to learn about simple machines, angles, patterns, perimeters, and so forth. The students that were allowed to create, problem solve, and collaborate extensively with great materials within real-life contexts will be able to make strong connections with those abstract concepts because they can tap into those kinesthetic, linguistic, and cognitive experiences. This is why active learning is so valuable for young children's future academic success, as it teaches students to learn for understanding through ongoing revisiting and refining of ideas, perspectives, and creations.

Inquiry-Based Math Learning

Your explicit awareness of the mathematical thinking and processing that the children are experiencing through their activities, and the intentionality with which you engage students with math-based inquiry is the distinguishing factor between the Mathematizing for Learning Process approach and other inquiry approaches. Your questioning patterns can be random, where interactions with children are decontextualized and unfocused. Or they can be intentional, where the questioning approach, content, types, and styles all align harmoniously to provide an in-depth instructional learning experience based on students' mathematical interests.

The processing involved in inquiry-based math learning can be a very demanding learning process for teachers. To be able to engage children in sustained and in-depth conversations, you have to be well equipped with knowledge and understanding of

- the material's transformational possibilities;
- the math language probabilities; and
- the metacognition and reflection elements utilized during inquiry sessions.

Teachers also have to rely heavily on their ability to ask in-depth mathematical questions during activities and projects. The questioning provided during these instances are intended to make children think about the mathematical processing they are investigating. The teacher's goal is to lead them to the understanding and truth of a concept through their own observations, conjectures, and generalizations. Incorporating inquiry-based math practices can be a cognitively demanding process, but a powerful and enjoyable practice when implemented with precision.

As the students become immersed in project-, problem-, and math-based learning processes, elements of planning and design (architecture) as well as problem, solution, and construction (engineering) are integrated to provide rigorous and meaningful learning experiences for children. It is active thinking and learning at its best, and it promotes children's participation in the construction of meaning process.

Collaborative and Cooperative Learning

The role of collaboration and cooperation in project-based learning is fundamental, as children and adults can collaborate on a shared goal or cooperate on common goals. However, "Preschoolers cannot become socially competent without many extended times to interact with one another" (Copple and Bredekamp 2010, 127), and students need opportunities to work as a social unit and develop holonomous communities, as "children learn a great deal in exchanges with their peers" (Gandini et al. 2008, 25), especially when they can interact in small groups. Well-thought-out projects provide wonderful opportunities for children to engage in group activities and conversations that can lead to the creation of children's theories and knowledge building, as well as the development of social and emotional competence, key elements of the social constructivist approach to learning.

Group effective facilitation processing is a fundamental practice that teachers can incorporate as they promote collaborative and cooperative learning. This process is the manner in which a teacher manages the group's involvement and thinking throughout the learning experiences. An important goal in the process is facilitating the group's ability to listen to members' points of view, with the goal of acknowledging students' responses as important contributions to the group's overall understanding. Just as important is the skill of facilitating the collective thinking and problem solving that occurs during collaborative-learning group sessions. When children are provided with many opportunities to engage intentionally with teachers who nurture perspective sharing and collaborative inquiry processing, they develop cognitively, linguistically, and socially. They also develop empathy for the process and each other. A dynamic and ethical community atmosphere develops in classrooms that establish these practices, setting the stage for active and higher-level learning.

Overall, understanding and being able to apply the science and art of inquiry within any educational setting is a complex procedure. Creating thinking and learning protocols, implementing project- and problem-based learning, and incorporating collaborative and cooperative practices as part of establishing metacognitive and reflective practice cultures are very demanding processes. These are skills and processes that take time to master. Nevertheless, they are well within reach for willing and committed teachers who work together to develop each other's pedagogical practices. Investing the time to understand the inquiry component of the Mathematizing for Learning Process approach provides a return on investment at an exponential rate as the teacher's and children's learning experiences are compounded infinitely. The rewards are endless.

6

Conclusion

The teaching of higher-level mathematics to young children is a challenging endeavor for any teacher. The Mathematizing for Learning Process approach framework organizes the complexity of the thinking required to teach meaningful mathematics to students, and this book showcases how the theoretical principles supported in the approach can be applied within early childhood settings. This approach supports teachers, in any educational setting, in their quest for teaching and facilitating children's learning through the use of emergent curriculum practices.

The processes of observation, exploration, language modeling, and inquiry are important skills that teachers can incorporate collectively in the process of architecting curriculum and instructional experiences for children. Through intentional planning and application, teachers can prepare themselves to engage students in higher-level learning processes that aim to develop mathematical and multidimensional thinking, the kind of thinking that allows children to build knowledge and develop understanding of the mathematical processes that exist within their contexts. It is through these higher-level experiences that teachers can combat the phenomenon of "inert knowledge," which is the process of knowing information without the understanding to apply it within a real-world setting.

The children that we teach and serve have the right to learn the mathematics that exists within their chosen fields, topics, and interests. Young children relate to us through their interactions with the classroom environments and the elements within them—their optimal learning contexts. Some of the fields within these contexts include architecture, engineering, culinary arts, creative arts, and literature, and the learning processes that they promote. These interests are clearly seen when children engage with blocks, water tools, cooking utensils, clay, and books. Mathematizing teachers can reduce any of these contexts to pure mathematical form and engage children in valuable learning experiences through processes that incorporate great materials, accurate language, and precise inquiry practices.

Teachers as well have the right to develop their pedagogical content knowledge and dispositions through systematic professional-learning communities and self-directed learning tools and resources that can help them achieve high instructional proficiency levels. As demonstrated throughout this book, teachers who have learned and implemented the Mathematizing for Learning Process approach have been given the experiences, knowledge, and tools to develop their teaching skills. They have also been provided with quantitative and qualitative data to support their ability to self-analyze and self-modify their teaching practices. Educators can utilize the methods, strategies, and techniques found throughout the book to increase their capacity to engage children in purposeful interactions and to establish *micro-math cultures* (environments where children's daily experiences are mathematized). Purposeful teachers know the *what*, *how*, and *why* of a learning experience and can sustain in-depth conversations with students during an interaction. Classrooms that have established micro-math cultures mathematize the routines, transitions, activities, explorations, and investigations that students can encounter on a daily basis. Micro-math-cultured classrooms embed mathematical learning in every aspect of the children's lives, providing them with maximum exposure to high-quality math experiences.

As stated in the beginning of the book, the MLP approach combines ideas and processes from multidisciplinary fields of learning in an attempt to create a holistic approach to learning mathematics. The wisdom learned from mathematicians, artists, architects, neuroscientists, and others across diverse fields provided the inspiration needed to think creatively and constructively about the best and most respectful ways of teaching math to young children.

Based on the blending and braiding of the multidisciplinary processes, teachers and children have been able to engage in short- and long-term studies and projects that have yielded wonderful results. Some of the positive results for teachers include

- increased observational skills (in math and other subject areas);
- a deeper understanding of the transformational possibilities of materials;
- the development of math grammar; and
- the ability to engage children in more intentional and precise mathematical experiences.

As for the children, the action and learning photos in this book tell the story. Students have been able to

- construct meaning of the mathematical concepts they have chosen to investigate and that are close to their hearts;
- create complex structures/compositions with creative and constructive materials through ongoing engagement, reflection, and refinement;
- acquire an extensive math vocabulary base;
- develop personal relationships with teachers and students through the collaborative inquiry process; and
- learn to think creatively and critically about math.

Further achievements from implementing the Mathematizing for Learning Process approach include the attainment of a 4-Star designation from the Quality Rating System of Illinois at two of the Christopher House early learning centers in Chicago, where I was the education director for fifteen years. At the time I wrote this book, the two centers joined the ranks of only five other early childhood institutions in Illinois with the highest designation, the Christopher House centers being the only two with Head Start programming. This approach also helped many teachers obtain high instructional scores on the Classroom Assessment Scoring System (CLASS) and on the Environmental Ratings Scales (ECERS/ITERS). Through the proficiency and confidence the teachers acquired, many were able to present their mathematizing skills nationally and regionally at the National Association for the Education of Young Children and the Chicago Metro Association for the Education of Young Children conferences. And, of course, the creation of this book provides the means to support teachers in their journey of developing professionally as the great teachers of our time.

It is my sincere hope that educators experience the joy of mathematizing children's experiences within any educational setting, and that they embrace the rich environments and atmospheres that develop through the implementation of this approach. Thank you for reading this book, and remember that mathematizing is the early childhood way.

GLOSSARY

Attributes: An observable characteristic or feature that describes a person or physical property.

Bilingual education: A systematic instructional approach that supports culturally and linguistically diverse students in the process of learning content and language through culturally relevant experiences.

Cognition: The use of mental processing to acquire knowledge and understanding.

Cognitive autonomy: The ability of an individual to think, evaluate, judge, and make decisions independently.

Cognitive conflict: A mental conflict that arises when new ideas or facts about something are in opposition to an individual's prior knowledge or understanding.

Cognitive flexibility: The ability of an individual to self-evaluate and self-modify their own thinking and behaviors.

Cognitive scaffolding: The process of supporting and extending a person's thinking and learning by providing materials meant to support problem solving, reasoning, and deeper levels of understanding.

Collaboration: A joint effort among a group of individuals who create shared goals and work together to achieve specific objectives.

Constructivism learning theory: A theory of learning based on the premise that individuals acquire knowledge and construct meaning of the world around them by reflecting on experience, internalizing the learning, and adapting the new information to a person's pre-existing understanding or mental structures.

Context: The environmental and sociocultural conditions in which someone lives or where something takes place.

Creative thinking: The mental process of generating ideas and combining elements with the purpose of forming new structures, functions, or entities.

Critical thinking: The mental process of examining a form of knowledge, testing its validity, and interpreting its meaning based on well-reasoned conclusions.

Direct math processing: The mind's mental mathematical activity that occurs as individuals are focused on a specific math concept within a task or experience. Math processing occurs as children create things with materials, and it is considered "direct" if a math concept was a focal point in the learning experience.

Emergent curriculum: A learner-centered curriculum in which educators plan learning experiences based on children's interests and sociocultural backgrounds.

Exploration of materials: The act of examining the properties of materials and the investigation of how those properties can be used to create, represent, and play.

Higher-level thinking: Mental processing that takes information and uses the intellectual behavior of analyzing, evaluating, and creating to make sense of the facts obtained.

Holistic integrated projects: Learning projects that incorporate the creative and critical modes of thinking to engage students in ongoing, sustained, and in-depth learning experiences.

Holonomous communities: A group that functions congruently, constructively, and productively within a collaborative learning context.

Holonomy: The idea that a person exists as both an autonomous individual and as a part of a whole, within a dynamic group organization.

Indirect math processing: The mind's mental mathematical activity that occurs indirectly of a person's conceptual focus during a task or experience. Math processing occurs as children create things with materials; however, it is considered "indirect" if a math concept was not the focus of the experience.

Inquiry: The process of examining facts through questioning, for the purpose of obtaining knowledge or solving a problem.

Learning modalities: The four types of sensations—auditory (hearing), visual (seeing), tactile (touching), and kinesthetic (moving)—that individuals use to construct meaning in the learning process.

Mathematize: The process of understanding the math cognitive and linguistic processing occurring within the contexts of children's daily lives.

Metacognition: The process of planning, monitoring, and evaluating a task before, during, or after an experience as a strategy for solving problems strategically.

Micro-math cultures: Environments where mathematical learning is embedded in every aspect of children's lives for the purpose of providing them with maximum exposure to high-quality math experiences.

Modular thinking: The mental process of thinking in standard units and dimensions for the purpose of producing structures or functional creations.

Multidimensional thinking: Visualizing problems from various angles and using different perspectives and types of thinking to find solutions.

Physical properties: Observable characteristics of substances that can be measured.

Progressive education: An educational perspective that emphasizes active learning, critical thinking, collaboration, and social justice as elements of a democratic environment focused on developing children's full potential and productive citizens of a community.

Proof: The act of establishing the validity of a hypothesis or mathematical conjecture through logical steps that lead to a factual conclusion.

Protocols: A multistep sequence of learning experiences that scaffold students' actions and thinking processes based on their interests and ideas.

Reflective practice: A way of reflecting upon experience for the purpose of learning how to improve our practices.

Reggio Emilia approach: An early childhood educational approach, originating from the Italian city of Reggio Emilia, that sees children as active citizens of a community, competent thinkers and constructors of their own understanding, and researchers on the path of exploring their environments. The approach emphasizes children's creativity, collaboration, and relationships through beautifully designed classrooms, long-term projects/studies, and representational work that challenges students to think critically about the world and their role in society.

Representation: Children's works of art that represent the thinking, experiences, or feelings the students are processing at the moment.

Social constructivism: A theory that children learn by engaging in collaborative processes with other individuals and their environment.

Topological thinking: The process of thinking with shapes, form, and space for the purpose of creating works of art.

BIBLIOGRAPHY

Anderson, Lorin W., David R. Krathwohl, Peter W. Airasian, Kathleen A. Cruikshank, Richard E. Mayer, Paul R. Pintrich, James Raths, Merlin C. Wittrock, and 6 more. 2000. *A Taxonomy for Learning, Teaching, and Assessing: A Revision of Bloom's Taxonomy of Educational Objectives, Complete Edition,* 1st Edition, 31. Adapted by permission of Pearson Education, Inc., Upper Saddle River, NJ.

Andrews, Angela, and Paul R. Trafton. 2002. *Little Kids—Powerful Problem Solvers: Math Stories from a Kindergarten Classroom.* Portsmouth, NH: Heinemann.

Ayas, Karen and Nick Zeniuk. 2001. "Project-based Learning: Building Communities of Reflective Practitioners." *Management Learning* 32 (1): 61–76.

Baker, Colin. 2011. *Foundations of Bilingual Education and Bilingualism*, 5th ed. Tonawanda, NY: Multilingual Matters.

Ball, Deborah L. 1988. "Knowledge and Reasoning in Mathematical Pedagogy: Examining What Prospective Teachers Bring to Teacher Education." PhD diss., Michigan State University, Lansing. Retrieved on October 10, 2012, from http://www-personal.umich.edu/~dball/books/DBall_dissertation.pdf.

Barnett, Steven W. 2008. "Preschool Education and Its Lasting Effects: Research and Policy Implications." Boulder, CO, and Tempe, AZ: Education and the Public Interest Center & Education Policy Research Unit. Retrieved September 25, 2012, from http://nepc.colorado.edu/files/PB-Barnett-EARLY-ED_FINAL.pdf.

Bates, Elizabeth. 1976. *Language and Context: The Acquisition of Pragmatics.* New York: Academic Press.

Bloom, Benjamin S. 1956. *Taxonomy of Educational Objectives: The Classification of Educational Goals. Handbook I: Cognitive Domain.* New York: David McKay Company.

Boals, Tim. 2001. "Ensuring Academic Success: The Real Issue in Educating English Language Learners." *Midwest Educational Research Journal* 14 (4): 3–8.

Bodrova, Elena and Leong, Deborah J. 2007. *Tools of the Mind: The Vygotskian Approach to Early Childhood Education*, 2nd ed. Columbus, OH: Merrill/Prentice Hall.

Bredekamp, Sue. 2003. "Standards for Preschool and Kindergarten Mathematics Education." *Engaging Young Children in Mathematics: Standards for Early Childhood Mathematics Education*, edited by Douglas H. Clements, Julie Sarama, and Ann-Marie DiBiase, 77–82. Mahwah, NJ: Erlbaum.

Bruner, Jerome S. 1961. "The Act of Discovery." *Harvard Educational Review* 31 (1): 21–32.

———. 1975. "Language as an Instrument of Thought." In *Problems of Language and Learning*, edited by Alan Davies, 66–88. London: Heinemann.

———. 1976. *The Process of Education*, rev. ed. Cambridge, MA: Harvard University Press.

———. 1978. "The Role of Dialogue in Language Acquisition." *The Child's Conception of Language*, edited by A. Sinclair, R. J. Jarvella, and W. J. M. Levelt, 241–56. New York: Springer-Verlag.

———. 1983. *Child's Talk: Learning to Use Language.* Oxford, England: Oxford University Press.

———. 1986. *Actual Minds, Possible Worlds.* Cambridge, MA: Harvard University Press.

Bruner, Jerome S., and Helen Haste. 1987. *Making Sense: The Child's Construction of the World*. New York: Methuen.

Carpenter, Thomas P., Elizabeth Fennema, Megan L. Franke, Linda Levi, and Susan B. Empson. 1999. *Children's Mathematics: Cognitively Guided Instruction*. Portsmouth, NH: Heinemann.

Carreón-Sánchez, Sulema. 2005. "Building Academic Language in Mathematics for English Learners." Paper presented at the Mathematics for English language Learners 2005 Conference. San Antonio, TX. Retrieved July 7, 2013, from http://www.tsusmell.org/downloads/Conferences/2005/Carreon-Sanchez_2005.pdf.

Carter, Susan. 2008. "Disequilibrium and Questioning in the Primary Classroom—Establishing Routines That Help Children Learn." *Teaching Children Mathematics* 15 (3): 134–37.

Chalmers, Christina. 2009. "Group Metacognition During Mathematical Problem Solving." Queensland, Australia: University of Technology. Retrieved July 10, 2013, from http://www.merga.net.au/documents/Chalmers_RP09.pdf.

Chomsky, Noam. 1965. *Aspects of the Theory of Syntax.* Cambridge, MA: MIT Press.

Clements, Douglas H., and Michael T. Battista. 1990. "Constructivist Learning and Teaching." *Arithmetic Teacher* 38 (1): 34–35.

Clements, Douglas H., and Julie Sarama. 2009. *Learning and Teaching Early Math: The Learning Trajectories Approach.* New York: Routledge.

———. 2014. "Play, Mathematics, and False Dichotomies." *Preschool Matters . . . Today!* (blog). Retrieved March 21, 2014, from http://preschool matters.org/2014/03/03/play-mathematics-and-false-dichotomies/.

Clements, Douglas H., Julie Sarama, and Ann-Marie DiBiase. 2004. *Engaging Young Children in Mathematics: Standards for Early Childhood Mathematics Education*. Mahwah, NJ: Erlbaum.

Cohen, Elaine P., and Ruth S. Gainer. 1995. *Art, Another Language for Learning*. Portsmouth, NH: Heinemann.

Collier, Virginia P. 1989. "How Long? A Synthesis of Research on Academic Achievement in a Second Language." *TESOL Quarterly* 23 (3): 509–31.

Comune di Reggio Emilia. 1987. *To Make a Portrait of a Lion*. Washington, DC: Distributed by Reggio Children USA. Videocassette.

Copley, Juanita V. 2001. "The Early Childhood Mathematics Collaborative: Communities of Discourse." *Teaching Children Mathematics* 8 (2): 100–103. Reston, VA: National Council of Teachers of Mathematics.

———. 2010. *The Young Child and Mathematics*, 2nd ed. Washington DC: National Association for the Education of Young Children. Jointly published by National Council of Teachers of Mathematics.

Copple, Carol E. 2004. "Mathematics Curriculum in the Early Childhood Context." In *Engaging Young Children in Mathematics: Standards for Early Childhood Mathematics Education*, edited by Douglas H. Clements, Julie Sarama, and Ann-Marie DiBiase, 83–87. Mahwah, NJ: Erlbaum.

Copple, Carol, and Sue Bredekamp. 2010. *Developmentally Appropriate Practice in Early Childhood Programs Serving Children from Birth through Age 8*, 3rd ed. Washington, DC: National Association for the Education of Young Children.

Costa, Arthur L., Robert J. Garmston, Robert H. Anderson, and Carl D. Glickman. 2002. *Cognitive Coaching: A Foundation for Renaissance Schools*, 2nd ed. Norwood, MA: Christopher-Gordan.

Costa, Arthur L., Kalaheo Hawaii, and Laura Lipton. 1999. *Holonomy: Paradox and Promise*. Yorktown, New York.

Cross, Christopher T., Taniesha A. Woods, and Heidi Schweingruber. 2009. *Mathematics Learning in Early Childhood: Paths Toward Excellence and Equity*. Washington, DC: National Academies Press.

Cummins, Jim. 1981. *The Role of Primary Language Development in Promoting Educational Success for Language Minority Students: A Theoretical Framework*. Los Angeles: National Dissemination Center.

———. 2000. *Language, Power, and Pedagogy: Bilingual Children in the Crossfire*. Tonawanda, NY: Multilingual Matters.

Curtis, Deb, and Margie Carter. 2007. *Learning Together with Young Children: A Curriculum Framework for Reflective Teachers.* St. Paul, MN: Redleaf Press.

DeVries, Rheta, and Constance Kamii. 2001. *Developing Constructivist Early Childhood Curriculum: Practical Principles and Activities.* New York: Teachers College Press.

———. 2011. *Ramps and Pathways: A Constructivist Approach to Physics with Young Children.* Washington, DC: National Association for the Education of Young Children.

Dewey, John. 1933. *How We Think: A Restatement of the Relation of Reflective Thinking to the Educative Process.* New York: D. C. Heath.

———. 1938. *Experience and Education.* New York: Kappa Delta Pi.

Dickinson, David K., and Patton O. Tabors. 2001. *Beginning Literacy with Language: Young Children Learning at Home and School.* Cambridge, MA: Brookes.

Echevarria, Jana J., MaryEllen Vogt, and Deborah J. Short. 2012. *Making Content Comprehensible for English Learners: The SIOP Model*, 4th ed. Upper-Saddle River, NJ: Pearson.

Edwards, Carolyn, Lella Gandini, and George Forman. 1998. *The Hundred Languages of Children: The Reggio Emilia Approach*, 2nd ed. West Port, CT: Ablex.

———. 2011. *The Hundred Languages of Children: The Reggio Emilia Approach—Advanced Reflections*, 3rd ed. Santa Barbara, CA: Praeger.

Eide, Brock, and Fernette Eide. 2006. *The Mislabeled Child: How Understanding Your Child's Unique Learning Style Can Open the Door to Success.* New York: Hyperion.

English, Lyn. 2011a. "Complex Learning through Cognitively Demanding Tasks" *Mathematics Enthusiast* 8 (3): 483–506.

———. 2011b. "Math and Complex Learning." *Curriculum Leadership* 9 (3): 1.

English, Lyn D., and Richard A. Lesh. 2003. "Ends-in-View Problems." In *Beyond Constructivism: A Models and Modelling Perspective on Mathematics Problem Solving, Learning, and Teaching,* edited by Richard A. Lesh and Helen Doerr, 297–316. Mahwah, NJ: Erlbaum.

Featherstone, Heather F., Sandra Crespo, Lisa M. Jilk, Joy A. Oslund, Amy N. Parks, and March B. Wood. 2011. *Smarter Together! Collaboration and Equity in the Elementary Classroom.* Reston, VA: National Council of Teachers of Mathematics.

Forman, George, and Brenda Fyfe. 2012a. "Negotiated Learning through Design, Documentation, and Discourse." In *The Hundred Languages of Children: The Reggio Emilia Experience in Transformation*, 3rd ed., edited by Carolyn Edwards, Lella Gandini, and George Forman, 247–71. Santa Barbara, CA: Praeger.

———. 2012b. "The Use of Digital Media in Reggio Emilia." In *The Hundred Languages of Children: The Reggio Emilia Experience in Transformation*, 3rd ed., edited by Carolyn Edwards, Lella Gandini, and George Forman, 343–55. Santa Barbara, CA: Praeger.

Fromboluti, Carol S., and Natalie Rinck. 1999. *Early Childhood: Where Learning Begins: Mathematics.* Washington, DC: US Department of Education Office of Educational Research and Improvement.

Galinsky, Ellen. 2010. *Mind in the Making: the Seven Essential Life Skills Every Child Needs,* 1st ed. New York: HarperCollins.

Gandini, Lella. 1993. "Fundamentals of the Reggio Emilia Approach to Early Childhood Education." *Young Children* 49 (1): 4–8.

Gandini, Lella, Lynn Hill, Louise Cadwell, and Charles Schwall. 2005. *In the Spirit of the Studio: Learning from the Atelier of Reggio Emilia*. New York: Teachers College Press.

Gandini, Lella, Susan Etheredge, and Lynn Hill. 2008. *Insights and Inspirations from Reggio Emilia.* Worcester, MA: Davis Publication.

Gillies, Robyn M. 2007. *Cooperative Learning: Integrating Theory and Practice.* Los Angeles: SAGE Publications.

Ginsburg, Herbert P. 2006. "Mathematical Play and Playful Mathematics: A Guide for Early Education." In *Play=Learning: How Play Motivates and Enhances Children's Cognitive and Social-Emotional Growth*, edited by Dorothy G. Singer, Roberta M. Golinkoff, and Kathy Hirsh-Pasek. Oxford: Oxford University Press. Retrieved July 10, 2012, from http://udel.edu/~roberta/play/Ginsburg.pdf.

———. 2010. "Herbert P. Ginsburg on Misconceptions about Mastering Early Math." *Harvard Education Letter.* Retrieved July 10, 2012, from http://www.hepg.org/page/102.

Ginsburg, Herbert. P., Sun L. Lee, and Judi S. Boyd. 2008. "Mathematics Education for Young Children: What It is and How to Promote It." Society for Research in Child Development *Social Policy Report* 22 (1): 5. Retrieved on February 28, 2015, from http://www.srcd.org/sites/default/files/documents/22-1_early_childhood_math.pdf.

Goos, Merrilyn, Peter Galbraith, and Peter Renshaw. 2002. "Socially Mediated Metacognition: Creating Collaborative Zones of Proximal Development in Small Group Problem Solving." *Educational Studies in Mathematics* 49 (2): 193–223.

Gowers, Tim, June Barrow-Green, and Imre Leader, eds. 2008. "The Language and Grammar of Mathematics." *The Princeton Companion to Mathematics*, 8–16. Princeton, NJ: Princeton University Press. Retrieved on December 10, 2014, from http://press.princeton.edu/chapters/gowers/gowers_I_2.pdf.

Gramlich, Jo Ann. 2001. "Talking to Your Child." *Montessori Life* 13 (1): 7.

Hakuta, Kenji., Yuko G. Butler, and Daria Witt. 2000. *How Long Does It Take English Language Learners to Develop Oral Proficiency and Academic Proficiency in English?* Stanford, CA: University of California Linguistic Minority Research Institute.

Hannon, Charles, and Diane J. Cook. 2000. *A Parallel Approach to Modeling Language Learning and Understanding in Young Children.* Arlington: University of Texas.

Harris, Robert. 1998. "Introduction to Creative Thinking." Retrieved on December 10, 2013, from http://www.virtualsalt.com/crebook1.htm.

Hart, Betty, and Todd Risley. 1995. *Meaningful Differences in the Everyday Experiences of Young American Children.* Baltimore, MD: Brookes.

———. 2003. "The Early Catastrophe. The 30 Million Word Gap by Age 3." *American Educator* 27 (1): 4–9.

Helm, Judy H., and Lilian G. Katz. 2010. *Young Investigators: The Project Approach in the Early Years*, 2nd ed. New York: Teachers College Press.

Herrmann, Ned. 2008. *The Creative Brain.* Lake Lure, NC: Ned Herrmann Group.

Hiebert, James, Thomas P. Carpenter, Elizabeth Fennema, Karen Fuson, Diane Wearne, and Hanlie Murray. 1997. *Making Sense: Teaching and Learning Mathematics with Understanding.* Portsmouth, NH: Heinemann.

Hiebert, James, and Patricia Lefevre. 1986. "Conceptual and Procedural Knowledge in Mathematics: An Introductory Analysis." *Conceptual and Procedural Knowledge: The Case of Mathematics*, edited by J. Hiebert, 1–27. Hillsdale, NJ: Erlbaum.

Hill, Heather C., Brian Rowan, and Deborah L. Ball. 2005. "Effects of Teachers' Mathematical Knowledge for Teaching on Student Achievement." *American Educational Research Journal* 42 (2): 371–401.

Hill, Lynn T., Andrew J. Stremmel, and Victoria Fu. 2005. *Teaching as Inquiry: Rethinking Curriculum in Early Childhood Education.* Columbus, OH: Pearson/Allyn and Bacon.

Hinsz, Verlin B. 2004. "Metacognition and Mental Models in Groups: An Illustration with Metamemory of Group Recognition Memory." In *Team*

Cognition: Understanding the Factors That Drive Process and Performance, edited by Salas Eduardo and Stephen M. Fiore, 33–58. Washington, DC: American Psychological Association.

Hoff, Erika, Marisol Parra, and Cynthia Core. 2010. "Relations among Language Exposure, Phonological Memory, and Language Development in Spanish-English Bilingually Developing 2-Year-Olds." *Journal of Experimental Child Psychology* 108 (1): 113–125.

Honig, Alice S. 1989. "Talk, Read, Joke, Make Friends: Language Powers for Children." *Day Care and Early Education* 16 (4): 14–17.

———. 1999. "Language Flowering, Language Empowering for Young Children." Paper presented at the Annual Meeting of the National Association for the Education of Young Children, New Orleans, LA, November 15–18, 1999. Retrieved on August 3, 2013, from http://files.eric.ed.gov/fulltext/ED437220.pdf.

Johnson, David W., and Frank P. Johnson. 2012. *Joining Together: Group Theory and Group Skills*, 11th ed. Harlow, England: Pearson.

Kamii, Constance, and Linda L. Joseph. 2003. *Young Children Continue to Reinvent Arithmetic: Implications of Piaget's Theory*, 2nd ed. New York: Teachers College Press.

Klibanoff, Raquel S., Susan C. Levine, Janellen Huttenlocher, Marina Vasilyeva, and Larry V. Hedges. 2006. "Preschool Children's Mathematical Knowledge: The Effect of Teacher 'Math Talk.'" *Developmental Psychology* 42 (1): 59–69.

Lampert, Magdalene, and Merrie L. Blunk. 1998. *Talking Mathematic: Studies of Teaching and Learning in School.* New York: Cambridge University Press.

Lane, Holly B., and Stephanie A. Allen. 2010. "The Vocabulary-Rich Classroom: Modeling Sophisticated Word Use to Promote Word Consciousness and Vocabulary Growth." Reading Rockets (website). Retrieved on December 12, 2013, from http://www.readingrockets.org/article/40991/.

Lee, Joon Sun, and Herbert P. Ginsburg. 2009. "Early Childhood Teachers' Misconceptions about Mathematics Education for Young Children in the United States." *Australasian Journal of Early Childhood* 34 (4): 37–45.

Leonard, Jacqueline, and Nora Ramirez. 2009. "Mathematizing for Empowerment." *NCTM News Bulletin.* Retrieved on October 10, 2012, from http://www.nctm.org/news/content.aspx?id=22964.

Lyman, Lawrence, and Harvey C. Foyle. 1988. "Cooperative Learning Strategies and Children." *Eric Digest.* Identifier: ED306003. Retrieved on March 7, 2013, from http://www.ericdigests.org/pre-9211/cooperative.htm.

Malaguzzi, Loris. 1994. "A Bill of Three Rights." North American Reggio Emilia Alliance. Retrieved on January 10, 2012, from http://www.reggioalliance.org/downloads/v2.n1.rights.pdf.

Manouchehri, Azita, and Dennis St. John. 2006. "From Classroom Discussion to Group Discourse." *Mathematics Teacher* 99 (8): 544.

Martens, Mary Lee. 1999. "Productive Questions: Tools for Supporting Constructivist Learning." *Science and Children* 36 (8): 24–27, 53.

McCray, Jennifer S., and Jie Q. Chen. 2012. "Pedagogical Content Knowledge for Preschool Mathematics: Construct Validity of a New Teacher Interview." *Journal of Research in Childhood Education* 26 (3): 291–307.

Montie, Jeanne E., Jill Claxton, and Shannon D. Lockhart. 2007. "A Multinational Study Supports Child-Initiated Learning: Using the Findings in Your Classroom." *Young Children* 62 (6): 22–26.

Moran, Mary J. 1998. "The Project Approach Framework for Teacher Education: A Case for Collaborative Learning and Reflective Practice." In *The Hundred Languages of Children: The Reggio Emilia Experience in Transformation*, 2nd ed., edited by Carolyn Edwards, Lella Gandini, and George Forman, 405–18. Westport, CT: Ablex.

National Association for the Education of Young Children (NAEYC) and the National Council of Teachers of Mathematics. 2010. "Early Childhood Mathematics: Promoting Good Beginnings." Retrieved July 10, 2014, from http://www.naeyc.org/files/naeyc/file/positions/psmath.pdf.

National Council of Teachers of Mathematics. 2000. "Principles and Standards for School Mathematics." Reston, VA: NCTM.

National Research Council. 1989. *Everybody Counts: A Report to the Nation on the Future of Mathematics Education*. Washington, DC: National Academy Press.

———. 1990. *Reshaping School Mathematics: A Philosophy and Framework for Curriculum*. Washington, DC: National Academy Press.

Nemeth, Karen N. 2009. *Many Languages, One Classroom: Teaching Dual and English Language Learners*. Silver Springs, MD: Gryphon House.

Opitz, Michael F., and Lindsey M. Guccione. 2009. *Comprehension and English Language Learners: 25 Oral Reading Strategies That Cross Proficiency Levels*. Portsmouth, NH: Heinemann.

Orlich, Donald C., Robert J. Harder, Richard C. Callahan, Michael S. Trevisan, and Abbie H. Brown. 2012. *Teaching Strategies; A Guide to Effective Instruction*, 10th ed. Belmont, CA: Cenage Learning.

Paul, Richard and Linda Elder. 2006. "Critical Thinking: Concepts and Tools." The Foundation For Critical Thinking. Retrieved February 24, 2014 from http://www.criticalthinking.org

———. 2009. *The Miniature Guide to Critical Thinking Concepts and Tools.* Dillon Beach, CA: Foundation for Critical Thinking Press.

Piaget, Jean. 1936. *Origins of Intelligence in the Child.* London: Routledge and Kegan Paul.

———. 1962. *Play, Dreams and Imitation*, vol. 24. New York: Norton.

———. 1964. *The Early Growth of Logic in a Child.* London: Routledge and Kegan Paul.

———. 1984. *Principles of Genetic Epistemology.* London: Routledge and Kegan Paul.

———. 1985. *The Equilibration of Cognitive Structures: The Central Problem of Intellectual Development.* Chicago: University of Chicago Press.

———. 2001. *The Language and Thought of the Child.* London: Routledge.

Rankin, Baji. 1998. "Curriculum Development in Reggio Emilia: A Long-Term Curriculum Project about Dinosaurs." In *The Hundred Languages of Children: The Reggio Emilia Experience in Transformation*, 2nd ed., edited by Carolyn Edwards, Lella Gandini, and George Forman, 215–37. Westport, CT: Ablex.

Reason, Peter, and Hillary Bradbury-Huang. 2008. *The SAGE Handbook of Action Research: Participative Inquiry and Practice*, 2nd ed. Thousand Oaks, CA: SAGE Publications.

Richardson, Kathy. 2003. "Making Sense." In *Engaging Young Children in Mathematics: Standards for Early Childhood Mathematics Education*, edited by Douglas H. Clements, Julie Sarama, and Ann-Marie DiBiase, 321–24. Mahwah, NJ: Erlbaum.

Rinaldi, Carlina. 2006. *In Dialogue with Reggio Emilia: Listening, Researching and Learning.* New York: Routledge.

Ritchhart, Ron, Mark Church, and Karin Morrison. 2011. *Making Thinking Visible: How to Promote Engagement, Understanding, and Independence for All Learners.* San Francisco: Jossey-Bass.

Rittenhouse, Peggy S. 1998. "The Teacher's Role in Mathematical Conversation: Stepping In and Stepping Out." In *Talking Mathematics in School: Studies of Teaching and Learning*, edited by Magdalene Lampert and Merrie L. Blunk, 163–89. Cambridge, MA: Cambridge University Press.

Rudd, Loretta C., Matthew C. Lambert, Macy Satterwhite, and Amai Zaier. 2008. "Mathematical Language in Early Childhood Settings: What Really Counts?" *Early Childhood Education Journal* 36 (1): 75–80.

Sarama, Julie and Douglas H. Clements. 2009a. "Building Blocks and Cognitive Building Blocks: Playing to Know the World Mathematically." *American Journal of Play* 1 (3): 313–37. Retrieved on February 5, 2013, from http://www.journalofplay.org/sites/www.journalofplay.org/files/pdf-articles/1-3-article-building-blocks-cognitive-building-blocks.pdf.

———. 2009b. *Early Childhood Mathematics Education Research: Learning Trajectories for Young Children.* New York: Routledge.

Scarcella, Robin. 2003. *Accelerating Academic English: A Focus on the English Learner.* Irvine, CA: University of California–Irvine.

———. 2008. *Academic Language and English Language Learners.* Webcast July 23, 2008, on Colorín Colorado. Retrieved on July 10, 2012, from http://www.colorincolorado.org/webcasts/academiclanguage/.

Scheinfeld, Daniel R., Karen M. Haigh, and Sandra J. P. Scheinfeld. 2008. *We Are All Explorers: Learning and Teaching with Reggio Principles in Urban Settings.* New York: Teachers College Press.

Schoenfeld, Alan H. 1992. "Learning to Think Mathematically: Problem Solving, Metacognition, and Sense Making in Mathematics." *Handbook for Research on Mathematics Teaching and Learning,* edited by D. Grouws, 334–70. New York: MacMillan.

Schön, Donald A. 1983. *The Reflective Practitioner: How Professionals Think in Action.* London: Temple Smith.

———. 1996. *Educating the Reflective Practitioner: Toward a New Design for Teaching and Learning in the Professions.* San Francisco: Jossey-Bass.

Seo, Kyoung-Hye, and Herbert P. Ginsburg. 2003. "What is Developmentally Appropriate in Early Childhood Mathematics Education? Lessons from New Research." In *Engaging Young Children in Mathematics*, edited by Douglas H. Clements, Julie Sarama, and Ann-Marie DiBiase, 91–104. Mahwah, NJ: Erlbaum. Retrieved on July 12, 2013, from http://gse.buffalo.edu/org/conference/ConfWritings2/Ginsburg_Kyoung.pdf.

Shapiro, Edna K., and Nancy Nager. 2000. *Revisiting a Progressive Pedagogy: The Developmental Interaction Approach.* Albany, NY: State University of New York Press.

Sinclair, Anne, Robert J. Jarvella, and Willem J. M. Levelt. 1978. *The Child's Conception of Language.* New York: Springer-Verlag.

Solomon-Rice, Patti, and Gloria Soto. 2009. "Language Modeling as an Efficacious Early Language Intervention Approach with Young Children Demonstrating Complex Communication Needs." *Perspectives on Augmentative and Alternative Communication* 18 (1): 21–27.

Vecchi, Vea. 2010. *Art and Creativity in Reggio Emilia: Exploring the Role and Potential of Ateliers in Early Childhood Education.* New York: Routledge.

Vygotsky, Lev S. 1962. *Thought and Language.* New York: Wiley.

———. 1978. *Mind in Society.* Cambridge, MA: Harvard University Press.

———. 1987. "Thinking and Speech." *The Collected Works of L.S. Vygotsky, Volume 1: Problems of General Psychology,* edited by R.W. Rieber and A.S. Carton. New York: Plenum Press. (First published in 1934.)

Weiser, Ellen T. 2008. "Students Control Their Own Learning: A Metacognitive Approach." *Teaching Children Mathematics* 15 (2): 91–96.

Wellhousen, Karyn and Judith E. Kieff. 2001. *A Constructivist Approach to Block Play in Early Childhood.* New York: Thomson Delmar Learning.

Wood, Terry. 1998. "Alternative Patterns of Communication in Mathematics Classes: Funneling or Focusing?" In *Language and Communication in the Mathematics Classroom,* edited by Heinz Steinbring, Maria G. Bartolini Bussi, and Anna Sierpinska, 167–78. Reston, VA: National Council of Teachers of Mathematics.

Zawojewski, Judith S., Richard A. Lesh, and Lyn English. 2003. "A Models and Modeling Perspective on the Role of Small Group Learning Activities." In *Beyond Constructivism: A Models and Modeling Perspective on Problem Solving, Learning, and Teaching*, edited by Richard A. Lesh and Helen M. Doerr, 337–58. Mahwah, NJ: Erlbaum.

INDEX

academic language, 14, 51
Albany Park Community Center (Chicago), 23–24
Allen, Stephanie, 54
analyzing, in Bloom's Taxonomy of Learning Objectives, 98
applying, in Bloom's Taxonomy of Learning Objectives, 98
attention-focusing questions, 84

Banzer, David, 39–42, 55–57
Belmont-Cragin Early Childhood Center (Chicago), 3–4, 27
Bigollo, Leonardo Pisano (Fibonacci), 71–72
bilingual education models, 13
Bloom, Benjamin, 14–15, 98
bridge study and project, 39–42
Bruner, Jerome, 97

Carole Robertson Center for Learning (Chicago), 36
Carrasquillo, Rosalinda, 23–24
Chambers, Meredith, 21, 73
Chicago Art Institute's Lion learning experience, 32–34
children, as self-guided learners, 38
children ages birth through three, importance of observing physical movements and actions, 20–21
Chinese American Service League Center (Chicago), 73
Christopher House early learning centers (Chicago), 117
clay
    as creative material, 25–26
    learning experiences using, 18, 29–34, 36, 39–42

Clements, Douglas H., 7
close-ended questions, 82
cognition, defining, 70
cognitive autonomy, 79
cognitive conflict
    challenge approach producing, 88–90
    described, 21
    incorporating with materials available, 20
cognitive flexibility, 79, 90
cognitive scaffolding
    described, 21
    focus and sustained interest, 23
    incorporating with materials available, 20
collaboration
    benefits of, 15
    higher-level thinking skills and, 95
    holistic integrated projects
        bridge project, 73–75
        Fibonacci Spiral, 71–72
        goal, 71
    importance of, 113–114
    reflective practice and, 15, 95
Collentine, Sarah, 54
comparative-thinking activities, example of, 14
comparison questions, 85
conceptualization, 62
construction-of-meaning process, 6–7
constructive materials, described, 25
constructivist education models
    children choose own learning contexts, 13
    collaboration, 15
    example of inquiry interaction, 88–90
    focusing approach, 79–80
    funneling approach and, 78
    project-based learning, 111–112
    proof skills, 92–94

135

teacher's characteristics, 76
See also problem solving, reasoning, and proof skills development
content language, 62
conversation language skills, developing, 52–53
conversations
    meaningful and ongoing, 63–64
    sustained and in-depth, 64
cooperation. *See* collaboration
creating, in Bloom's Taxonomy of Learning Objectives, 98
creative materials, described, 25
creative thinking
    defining, 71
    multidimensional thinking and, 38
    opera house drawings example, 92–94
    role-playing and, 29, 91
    stimulating with holistic integrated projects, 71–72, 73–75
critical thinking
    defining, 71
    multidimensional thinking and, 38, 39
    opera house drawings example, 92–94
    stimulating with holistic integrated projects, 71–72, 73–75
    use of Bloom's taxonomy, 14–15
curiosity
    exploration and, 29
    importance of, 28
    instilling, 29
        Chicago Art Institute's Lion learning experience, 32–34
        San Prospero Lion learning experience, 29–32

developmental approach, children choose own learning contexts, 13
digital recording devices, using, 64
direct processing, 22–23
dual-language learners, importance of observing physical movements and actions, 20–21

Early Childhood Mathematics: Promoting Good Beginnings (NAEYC and NCTM), 64
elementary school children, mathematical language and concept continuum, 26, 27
emergent math curriculums
    basis, 17
    teacher as facilitator, 55
    versus traditional skills-based approach, 6–7
environment
    elements, 17, 18
    for exploration, 26–27
    meaningful engagement with, by choosing own learning contexts, 13
    play experiences, 13
environmental mathematizing experiences
    building height, 5–7
    with containers, 2
    at supermarket, 1
    tree photograph, 7–8
evaluating, in Bloom's Taxonomy of Learning Objectives, 98
exploration with materials component
    clay
        as creative material, 25–26
        learning experiences using, 18, 29–34, 36, 39–42
    described, 11
    elements, 12
        developing multidimensional thinking skills, 37–42
        discovering physical properties and attributes of materials, 34–36
        instilling curiosity, 29–34
    environment, 26–27
    selecting materials, 28, 71
    types of materials, 25

Fibonacci Spiral, 71–72
Flynn-Rambo, Tyler, 97
focusing approach, 79–80
funneling approach, 78

Gambetti, Amelia, 29
glossary, 119–121
group effective facilitation, 114
group metacognition, 95–97

higher cognitive processing, 70
higher-level mathematical concepts
    described, 43
    integrating into classroom experiences, 44
higher-level thinking skills, group learning and collaboration, 95
high-frequency math words charts, 59–60
holistic integrated projects
    bridge project, 73–75
    Fibonacci Spiral, 71–72
    goal, 71
holonomous communities, 72, 113–114
holonomy, defined, 72
Honig, Alice, 53

income level and mathematical proficiency, 43
indirect processing, 22–23
inert knowledge, 115
infants and toddlers
    learning experiences with clay, 36
    mathematical language and concept continuum, 26, 27
information, construction of meaning, 13
initiation-response-feedback (IRF) approach, 76–78
inquiry component
    described, 11, 69
    elements, 12
        creating protocols for group metacognition and reflective practice, 95–97
        developing thinking protocols, 97–102
        implementing high-level questioning patterns to develop problem solving, reasoning, and proof skill. *See* problem solving, reasoning, and proof skills development
        learning protocols, 103–111
        promoting creative and critical thinking through holistic integrated projects, 70–75
    inquiry-based interaction, 88–90
    math-based, 112–113
    proof and reasoning language and questions, 62, 86
    proof skills, 92–94
intuitive thinking, 75

Jones, Jennifer, 70

Landt, Fran, 18–19
Lane, Holly, 54
language acquisition and development
    babbling, 52–53
    income level and, 43–44
    mathematical continuum, 26, 27
    during play, 14
    quantifying teacher's math language, 58–59
    using age-appropriate, 26
language modeling component
    described, 11
    elements, 12
        developing math grammar. *See* math grammar development
        engaging in ongoing, sustained, and in-depth conversations, 63–67
        expanding and extending language, 52–53
        labeling language, 52
        parallel talk, 53
        spiral talk, 54–55
    example, 55–57
    importance of, 43
    quantifying teacher's math language, 58–59
    of social and academic language, 14
    teacher's aids
        high-frequency math words charts, 59–60
        math content, reasoning, and proof charts, 61–63

math word family collaboration charts, 60–61
learning experiences
  bridge study and project, 39–42
  Chicago Art Institute's Lion, 32–34
  creating optimal, 17
  environmental
    building height, 5–7
    with containers, 2
    at supermarket, 1
    tree photograph, 7–8
  Fibonacci Spiral, 71–72
  kindergartners' measurement study, 65–67
  kingdom study (structure and function), 104–107, 110
  mathematical literature, 107–110
  opera house drawings, 92–94
  San Prospero Lion, 29–32
  theatre study, 99–102
  urban engineering study, 23–24
learning protocols
  defining, 103
  developing
    kingdom study (structure and function), 104–107, 110
    mathematical literature, 107–110
    scaffolding, 97
    teacher control and, 103
  scope, organization, and purpose, 110–111
Leonard, Jacqueline, 1
linguistic development, supporting while mathematizing, 2
logical-mathematical skills development, 13
logical thinking and constructive materials, 25
lower-level mathematical concepts, described, 43

Marten, Mary Lee, 84
materials
  developing multidimensional thinking skills, 37–42
  discovering physical properties and attributes, 34–36
  instilling curiosity, 29–34
  project- and problem-based learning and, 111–112
  selecting, 71
  types, 25
math anxiety, overcoming, 9
math content, reasoning, and proof charts, 61–63
mathematical physics in urban engineering study, 23–24
mathematize, definitions, 1
Mathematizing for Learning Process (MLP) approach
  components
    exploration. *See* exploration with materials component
    inquiry. *See* inquiry component
    language modeling. *See* language modeling component
    observation. *See* observation component
  distinguishing feature, 112–113
  overview, 2–3, 9, 12
  principles and values
    children choose own learning contexts, 12–13
    collaboration, 15–16
    critical thinking, 14–15
    importance of play, 13
    language acquisition and development, 14
  results, 116–117
  as static and dynamic, 16
math grammar development
  components, 51
  described, 44–45
  importance of, 44
  word lists
    adjectives, 47–49
    adverbs, 49–50
    content words, 45–46

money and business, 51
nouns, 46–47
prepositions and conjunctions, 50
verbs, 49
math word family collaboration charts, 60–61
metacognition, described, 95
metacognitive processing in collaborative process, 15
micro-math cultures, 1–2, 116
modularity, 25
Molina, Lourdes, 34
motivation, as catalyst, 29
multidimensional thinking skills
    bridge study and project, 39–42
    creative thinking elements, 38
    critical thinking elements, 38, 39
    higher cognitive processing, 70
    materials exploration, 37–38
    role-playing and, 38

National Association for the Education of Young Children (NAEYC), 64
National Council of Teachers of Mathematics (NCTM), 64

observation component
    described, 11
    elements, 12
        describing indirect and direct math processing, 22–23
        identifying children's environmental, role-playing, and representational contexts and interests, 17–19
        recognizing physical movements and actions, 20–21
open-ended questions, 82
opera house drawings, 92–94

parallel talk, 53
parent/child learning experiences
    in classroom, 4
    environmental
        building height, 5–7
        with containers, 2
        at supermarket, 1
        tree photograph, 7–8
personal knowledge and experiences, importance of, 17
physical movements and actions, recognizing, 20–21
physical properties and attributes of materials, 25, 34–36
Piaget, Jean, 97
play
    importance of, 13
    language acquisition and development during, 14
    time for exploratory, 35
    See also role-playing
preschoolers
    mathematical language and concept continuum, 26, 27
    mathematizing and linguistic development, 2
    rainbow investigation
probabilities, mathematizing, 5–7
problem solving, reasoning, and proof skills development
    examples of promoting, 88–91, 94
    materials and, 111–112
    proof skills, 92–94
    questioning approach
        content questioning, 80–82
        focusing, 79–80
        Questioning Patterns (ACTS) chart, 77
        Questioning Vortex, 76
        types of questions, 82–83, 84–87
productive questions
    styles, 84
        attention-focusing, 84
        comparison, 85
        problem-solving, 85
        professional development and, 87
        proof, 86
        quantifying, 85
        reasoning, 86

spatial relations, 85
   using, 84
project approach, 13, 111–112
proof language, 62
proof questions, 86
proof skills, 92–94
"provocatory" questioning, 111–112

quantifying questions, 85
questioning approach to develop problem solving, reasoning, and proof skills
   content questioning, 80–82
   focusing, 79–80
   Questioning Patterns (ACTS) chart, 76, 77
   Questioning Vortex, 76
   types of questions, 82–83, 84–87

rainbow investigation, 3–4
Ramirez, Nora, 1
reasoning language, 62
reasoning questions, 86
reflective practice
   collaboration and, 15
   creating protocols, 95–97
   described, 95
Reggio Emilia approach
   children choose own learning contexts, 12
   opera house drawings, 92–94
   San Prospero Lion learning experience, 29–32
remembering, in Bloom's Taxonomy of Learning Objectives, 98
representational contexts and interests
   identifying, 19
   multidimensional thinking and, 39
role-playing
   creative thinking and, 29, 91
   to develop multidimensional thinking skills, 38
   during play, 17, 18–19
   in theatre study thinking protocol, 99–101

San Prospero Lion learning experience, 29–32
Sarama, Julie, 7
social constructivism, 13
spatial relations questions, 85
spiral talk, 54–55

"Taxonomy of Educational Objectives" (Bloom), 14–15, 98
teacher-directed approach. *See* traditional skills-based approach
teacher's aids, language modeling
   high-frequency math words charts, 59–60
   math content, reasoning, and proof charts, 61–63
   math word family collaboration charts, 60–61
Teatro Municipale drawings, 92–94
thinking protocols
   defining, 97
   developing
      scaffolding, 97
      theatre study, 99–102
      using Bloom's Taxonomy of Learning Objectives, 97–98
   scope, organization, and purpose, 110–111
thinking skills
   constructive materials and logical, 25
   creative
      defining, 71
      multidimensional thinking and, 38
      opera house drawings example, 92–94
      role-playing and, 29, 91
      stimulating with holistic integrated projects, 71–72, 73–75
   critical
      defining, 71
      multidimensional thinking and, 38, 39
      opera house drawings example, 92–94
      stimulating with holistic integrated projects, 71–72, 73–75

use of Bloom's taxonomy, 14–15
defining, 70
group learning and collaboration, 95
intuitive, 75
multidimensional
    bridge study and project, 39–42
    creative thinking elements, 38
    critical thinking elements, 38, 39
    higher cognitive processing, 70
    materials exploration, 37–38
    role-playing and, 38
topological, 25
topological thinking, 25
traditional skills-based approach
    emergent math curriculums versus, 6–7
    funneling approach, 78
    initiation-response-feedback approach, 78
    language acquisition, 54–55
Tzontcheva, Snejana, 23

understanding, in Bloom's Taxonomy of Learning Objectives, 98

Van Schoyck, Tamara, 83
visual integrity, 18
vocabulary development. *See* language acquisition and development; language modeling component
Vygotsky, Lev, 97

Yañez, Erika, 65–67